GABRIEL OKARA

This book is dedicated to the

memory of my father,

Chief Samson Gbaingbain Okara,

who insisted that I "read book,"

so that my hands would not

be as rough as his own.

CONTENTS

ACKNOWLEDGMENTS

Works collected here appeared in previous volumes, and the author wishes to thank the publishers of those volumes, including Heinemann Educational Books, Ethiope Publishing, and Editions Rodopi, with special thanks to Chinyelu F. Ojukwu of University of Port Harcourt Press.

Thanks are due also to Professor Chukwuma Azuonye of the University of Massachusetts, Boston, for his encouragement and help in the early stages of preparation of the manuscript for this collection.

Especially invaluable in the completion of the current volume has been the steadfast support of my family, especially my son, daughter, and granddaughter, all of whom worked tirelessly to help see this work into publication. And so I express here my sincere gratitude to Ebi, Timinipre, and to Katja.

I would be remiss were I not to mention here the role of Government College, Umuahia, in my early, formative years and my life and work as a writer. For it was there that the habit of reading was cultivated in me.

My father, a chief and successful palm-produce entrepreneur, was, in his youth, also a wrestling champion. He worked with his hands. And it was he who insisted that I study and become an educated man.

— *Gabriel Okara*

INTRODUCTION

Brenda Marie Osbey

Dubbed the "Year of Africa," 1960 saw the liberation of seventeen sub-Saharan nations from European imperial and colonial rule. It was the culmination of African mass movements for independence stretching back nearly half a century and peaking during World War II, a war in which upwards of 350,000 African men and women served the cause of the Allied Forces.

Acknowledging the escalating continent-wide movement for independence and its inevitable achievement, on 10 January at Accra, capital of the newly independent Republic of Ghana, and again on 3 February at Cape Town, South Africa, British prime minister Harold Macmillan made his now famous "Wind of Change" speech. "It is happening everywhere," he cautioned. "The wind of change is blowing through this continent, and whether we like it or not, this growth of national consciousness is a political fact. We must all accept it as a fact, and our national policies must take account of it." The world's farthest-reaching empire thus capitulated to the irrepressible will of an Africa bent on self-governance.

On New Year's Day of independence year Langston Hughes had already published the first edition of *An African Treasury: Articles, Essays, Stories, Poems by Black Africans*. Compiled over a period of six years, it contains work by writers from every region. In his introduction Hughes writes of "a common yearning that may best be described by the stirring, concluding response at the Accra [All-African Peoples'] Conference: Mayibuye, Africa!

Freely translated, that means 'Long live Africa!' But the literal translation comes much closer: 'Come back, Africa!'" Evidence of his lifelong commitment to building literary bridges among people of African descent across the globe, this collection is, more specifically, a statement of Hughes's solidarity with Africa and Africans. "What white writers think of the once Dark Continent we long have known," he concludes. "These pages tell what black writers think."

Nigeria, which would remain a British colony until October of that year, is represented in the anthology by a half-dozen authors across genres. Included is a single poem by Gabriel Okara. In it we find early examples of a few of the poet's characteristic devices: figurative language that emphasizes tensions between past and future, tradition and change, Africa and the West; use of a persona who, as solitary observer of a changing landscape, scene or moment, reveals a philosophical tendency to weigh discrete and often conflicting views, circumstances, voices; the contemplative mood or tone that remains a key element of his current work. In five short stanzas, "Spirit of the Wind" reveals more than an awareness of coming change. The ringing of the angelus, whether at daybreak, noontime, or early evening, is the call to prayer in observance of the Annunciation of the coming of the Christian savior. Despite the midday bell, however, the solitary observer remains seated on his rock, grounded in the present moment. No savior arrives. Instead, the homing instinct of the storks awakens the solitary observer's "vital call," his own freedom instinct. But his prayer is in the form of a question directed to the state of his own stork, "caged / in Singed Hair and Dark Skin."

Gabriel Imomotimi Gbaingbain Okara was born 24 April 1921 into a noble family, the son of Ijaw chief and businessman Samson G. Okara and Martha Olodiama Okara, a homemaker. His birthplace, Bumoundi, was then part of the Yenagoa Local Government Area, since renamed Bayelsa State. The newer name is an acronym for the former Brass, Yenagoa, and Sagbama Local Government areas of British-occupied Nigeria. Situated in the Niger Delta, Bayelsa borders Delta State to the north, Rivers State to the east and the Atlantic Ocean to the southwest. Traditionally a fishing, maritime, farming and regional crafts economy, Bayelsa has been a key site in Nigeria's oil-producing industry since the 1950s, when exploratory drilling proved the entire area to be oil-rich. Since then, Nigeria has been the African continent's largest source of natural oil and gas, among the largest oil producers in the world. The oil fields are there in the Niger Delta, a dense natural landscape of rain forests, mangrove swamps, rivers, and a once thriving fishing industry. Ironically, the region had long before been referred to as the "Oil Rivers" because it was a major producer of *dendê*, or palm oil, traditionally used in cooking. Following British colonial control, palm oil became a major commodity, used in commercial food preparation, soapmaking (think Palmolive), and as an industrial-grade machine lubricant. With the discovery of crude oil there in early 1956 came the unrelenting drilling, blasting and burning into the air, or "flaring," of crude. And activism against the resulting pollution, environmental damage, disease and death, has been ongoing ever since. The local fishing economy was, of course, an immediate casualty of the oil boom. And a top-down policy was quickly established, in which oil royalties were collected by the federal government, ostensibly to be equally distributed across the nation. Yet the once thriving Delta, from which the nation's new oil wealth derived, became increasingly impoverished. Attempts by Delta communities to resolve combined environmental and economic woes through talks with oil company and government representatives were met first with indifference and then with violence. A new phase of community organizing began in the 1960s, but conditions in the Delta continued to worsen and continue to worsen now. By 1990, the poet Kenule "Ken" Beeson Saro-Wiwa had begun organizing peaceful protests in his native Ogoniland in Rivers State and across the Delta region against human rights and environmental abuses by multinational oil companies and denouncing the complicity of the government of military dictator Sani Abacha. Following multiple false arrests, imprisonment and sham trial, the government-ordered execution by hanging of Saro-Wiwa and eight other activists in a single day in November 1995 shocked local, national and international human and environmental rights advocates and raised international calls for sanctions against the oil corporations and the Abacha regime. At home in Ogoniland, the impact of Saro-Wiwa's murder was immediate, intimate and ongoing. In addition to the grief of family and fellow activists, the broader Niger Delta community as a whole was in mourning. "Self Preservation," Okara's poem in memory of the martyred poet-activist, carries the plainest subtitle and dedication: to "Ken Saro-Wiwa—Hanged Human Rights Campaigner." The opening lines lament the silencing of "yet unsounded drums of dormant hopes, questions" and the "compost heap of dead promises." Ogoni and Ijaw people have long been united not only by the environmental threats posed by the oil industry across their region, but also by shared land, history and cultural outlook.

The Niger Delta extends over twenty-five thousand square miles and is home to more than thirty million people belonging to nearly fifty ethnicities and speaking about 250 languages. The Ijaw, to whom it has been home for at least seven thousand years, are its oldest human presence, tracing their history to a time before time, when the people "fell from the skies."

Ijaw cosmology holds that prior to physical birth, human beings dwell for a time among water spirits. After departing that watery generative and dormative realm, and throughout earthly life, the people carry out specific rites, prayers and public observances including dance, song, masque dramas and processions in order to insure that their earthly community remains in harmony with the host spirits among whom they first lived. Religion and cultural tradition thus emphasize the necessity not only of maintaining balance between human and natural environments, but of active recognition and vigilance, contribution to and protection of the life-giving Delta. Traditionally, then, water, and rivers in particular, hold an appropriately sacred place in Ijaw identity and sensibilities. How fitting then that Okara's literary career should begin with "The Call of the River Nun." With publication of this first poem, Gabriel Okara would establish his literary identity firmly within the landscape and waterscape of the Delta. His body of work, in poetry and prose, is replete with riverine imagery and an abiding consciousness of union with the natural environment. Among the most anthologized works by any Nigerian poet, it has generally been interpreted as a poem of nostalgia, which may well have been the author's original intent. In the half-century since its publication, it has nevertheless become touchstone, prayer, protest and lyric anthem for the restoration and protection of the unified natural and human habitat of the Niger Delta.

If indeed the combined theme and mood of "The Call of the River Nun" is nostalgic, it is a nostalgia not only of "the ghost of a child / listening" but of the mature speaker anticipating that future when he will "watch / my mirrored self unfold." The river would thus appear to function as literal, figurative and projected reflector of human memory and desire. The speaker and the river, however, are far more intimately related. To read the river as mere setting or even place to which the speaker returns is to miss the most basic expression of this poem in which river and speaker call out and address *one another* in their shared, native riverine language, a language unique within the surrounding and related terrain.

The poem opens with the speaker's impassioned reply: "I hear your call! / I hear it far away; / I hear it break the circle / of these crouching hills." Each stanza is a more urgent reply, until the fourth and longest, when the speaker exclaims plainly, "My river's calling too!" The language of the poem — the English language in which the poet composes — is thus a translation of the mother tongue of river and man, who are not only interdependent, but are, in fact, kin.

Composed in 1950, "The Call of the River Nun" garnered the silver cup in poetry at the 1953 Nigerian Festival of the Arts at Lagos and was published in the 1957 inaugural issue of *Black Orpheus*, the first English-language journal of African literature. Indeed, it is with publication of Gabriel Okara's first poem that Nigerian literature in English and modern African poetry in this language can be said truly to have begun.

The generation of African poets immediately prior are the so-called pioneers in anglophone African poetry. Born in the first decades of the twentieth century, the better known among them are contemporaries of the youngest poets of the Harlem Renaissance, Langston Hughes and Helene Johnson; Négritude poets Guy Tirolien of Guadeloupe and Aimé Césaire of Martinique; and Cuban Négrismo founder Nicolás Guillén. The African pioneers were born, educated, grew to adulthood and pursued their literary vocations entirely under the banner of British colonial rule. They were, in effect, British. Their parents had converted to Christianity, worked in colonial civil service jobs and the professions, or else were independent and often wealthy merchants. They were the first generation to attain middle-class standing under colonial rule and to embrace British manners and social values. Because Great Britain had employed a policy of indirect rule in Africa, however, they did all of this in an African social and cultural environment. They then sent their children to be educated in England, where they would be perceived and routinely treated as members of an inferior racial minority and, quite possibly for the first time in their lives, be compelled to confront white racism on a daily basis. They rebelled. And many of this newly Western-educated generation chose poetry as the means to express their resistance to social marginalization, exclusion and racism. But the authors they studied at school were hardly worthy models. Tennyson and *Kipling*? The resulting body of verse is at best a constrained and regrettable amalgam of the religious zeal and regular meter of Protestant missionary hymnody and late Victorian attitudes of forbearance, rigidity and self-doubt. Despite the absence of direct models of modern literary style or diction in English, and their struggle to reconcile conflicting African and British identities, the first generation of anglophone African poets was nonetheless determined to assert race pride.

The best-known Nigerian poet of the period is Dennis Chukwude Osadebay (1911–94), a practicing lawyer and longtime political officeholder. The opening lines from his "Song of Hope" illustrate the influence of the hymnal:

Is thy weather rough and cruel,
Charged with thunder, dark and cold?
Does thy fire lack fuel
To thy heart great misery hold?
Look around, O woman's born,
Full many a soul by sorrow torn
From happiness and heaven's door
Is worse than thou on Fortune's floor.

A more promising effort is "Young Africa's Plea." Not only has the poet here retired his earlier dependence on rhyme and Christian preachments in favor of free verse and more natural voice and tone, he manages also to fashion a persona who begins by asserting the right to self-determination:

> Don't preserve my customs
> As some fine curios
> To suit some white historian's tastes.

As soon as the second stanza, however, Young Africa succumbs to self-doubt and can only appeal for time to sort matters through:

> Let me play with the whiteman's ways
> Let me work with the blackman's brains
> Let my affairs themselves sort out. . . .

It is easy enough to dismiss the early anglophone African poets for their lack of literary technique, their labored or stilted language, style and tone. But the same is true of the pioneer francophone Caribbean poets writing before the Négritude movement. Who remembers, for instance, the poems of Émile Roumer of Haiti? Or any poet from Guiana before Léon Damas? It is because the pioneers *were* the first to attempt poetry in English that they had no near or prior models for what African poetry in English could be. For that the literary world would have to wait for the first poems of Gabriel Okara.

The shortcomings of well-meaning versifiers like Osadebay are no doubt the origin of the tradition of treating Okara's work as belonging to the same generation as that of such later Nigerian poets as Christopher Okigbo, Wole Soyinka, John Pepper Clark Bekederemo, and Kofi Awoonor of Ghana. This is reasonable to the extent that poems by these five were frequently published in the same journals, magazines and anthologies. But the fact that these writers all are ten, fifteen or more years younger suggests that such a grouping is largely a matter of convenience for poetry scholars and literary historians. Rather than trying to fit Okara's work into the later period, it is more accurate to recognize that his poetry is at once a bridge to that of the younger writers with which it has been so often discussed, and an oeuvre unto itself. Simply put, Gabriel Okara is the first modern African poet.

Okara received primary schooling at home in Bumoundi and also at Kaiama. In 1935, when he was fourteen years old, he was admitted to Government College, Umuahia, an elite college preparatory high school, where he was a boarding student until the outbreak of World War II. The school became known as a literary incubator and would eventually include in its roster many future authors, including Okigbo, Achebe, Soyinka, and Saro-Wiwa. Matriculating in 1940, Okara was the first of many major writers to study at the Nigerian prep school known as the "Eton of the East."

Having been transformed in 1930 from teacher training institute to a modified version of the selective and academically rigorous English public school model, Umuahia was still new at the time of Okara's enrollment, and teachers were typically young and forward-looking. Boys attending Umuahia, and the even more prestigious King's College, Lagos, were expected to pursue university education and employment in the colonial civil service. They were encouraged to engage fully in the life of the school, to support one another in their studies and to participate in competitive sports like cricket and soccer. They pursued a university-level arts and sciences curriculum. Okara initially showed greater commitment to painting. But it was there at Umuahia that he first began to write.

Studies at Umuahia were interrupted by the advent of World War II and its students assigned to other schools after the site was commandeered as a detention camp for prisoners of war. Okara was transferred briefly to Yaba Higher College, located near Lagos. Yaba was at that time the highest educational institution in the country. And it was there that he sat for final examinations and received the Senior Cambridge School Certificate in 1940 before presenting himself for military service. Unable to pass the physical examination, however, he worked instead for British Airways. Following the war, he worked in civil service and then government publishing and bookbinding. Throughout this time, he continued reading and studying literature and writing both poetry and prose.

Okara is essentially a lyric poet. Which is to say that he is particularly committed to the musical, rhythmic capacities of language, and to finding the fit language to serve a given poem. His work in poetry and prose has a unity of voice, tone, inflection. Even his longer, narrative poems are keenly attuned to the transformative powers of language and are marked by a decidedly lyric accent, often relying on repetition of units of sound and line in the form of alliteration, chant, incantation.

Among the most poignant and compelling poems in the current volume are those written during the Biafran War for Independence, waged from July 1967 until January 1970. Many fighting for Biafra were students, artists and intellectuals, inexperienced at war but committed to the struggle for an independent homeland. And Okara served for the duration as head of cultural and information services on the side of the short-lived republic. During that time, he traveled frequently to Europe and the United States to gain support for the Biafran cause, sometimes on reading tours with Achebe and short story writer Cyprian Ekwensi. At home in his own country, physical safety was a primary concern. While he was away on one such tour, for instance, his family had to flee Umuahia, taking with them only as much as could be quickly loaded into their car. Such escapes were common during the war years. And personal effects and papers — poems, short stories, essays and a second novel — were lost as he and his family raced to escape fast-advancing Nigerian federal troops.

The poems from that period that survived comprised his first poetry volume, *The Fisherman's Invocation*, published in 1978. The title poem won Britain's 1979 Commonwealth Prize for best poem of the year — the first work by an African poet to do so. A narrative sequence in five numbered and titled cantos, it is among the longer poems in the present collection. It takes place on a river in the Niger Delta, and consists entirely in an extended dialogue between two men engaged in the traditional occupation of fishing.

Of the many poems characterized by riverine imagery, "The Fisherman's Invocation" thoroughly immerses the reader in the world of the Delta. Using such Ijaw language constructs as "Back" and "Front" to express past and future, Okara shapes such dialogue as "The Front grows from the Back / like buds from a tree stump" and "Do buds sprout from dead stumps? / The stump of my Back is standing dead." The first speaker is clearly confident in the power of history and traditional culture to pave the way for a new and progressive post-Independence nation; the second is burdened with doubt. "At the back of my Back," he admits, "I see only darkness / and the water in the desert / has dried in darkness." Courage is indicated in Ijaw not by speaking of the abstract quality, but of the chest which contains the human heart. To have a "strong chest," therefore, is to be brave, confident, forward-looking. When the second speaker admits that he has forgotten how to hope, the first firmly but patiently advises him how to proceed. Appearing to speak about the drawing up of fishing nets, the first speaker urges his compatriot, "Draw man draw / Strengthen your Chest."

Rather than viewing traditional culture as having only to do with the past, or the natural world of the Delta as mere setting against which the drama of life is performed, Okara, through his use of Ijaw syntax, religious symbology, proverbial speech and tone, reveals a commitment to the future of an independent and truly free Nigeria. He fully immerses the reader in an Ijaw philosophical worldview at the same time as he expresses faith in that eventual future.

There's water
there's water from a river
flowing from the bottom of the Back
of the womb. So draw up the Back caught
in the net. Draw it up and let's look it over
in our insides, in our heads

The Back is my first
little paddle I lost
in the river and whose
shape I cannot now remember

Then let your head
be the head of an elephant
let your eyes be the eyes
of a leopard and stalk the Back
stalk the Back in the forest
stalk the Back in the heavens
stalk it in the earth
stalk it in your umbilical cord.

The birthing language and imagery of the invocation is not entirely figurative. Such words and expressions as *womb, Back of the womb, breast, midwifemoon*, those passages where there is only *shape in the womb*, and his painterly renderings of the slow and bloody *birthing course* are translations of traditional religious concepts about the making of the physical world of the Niger Delta and its multiethnic culture and society. Because both the waters and the Ijaw creator deity are feminine, the mermaid-like figure of Mammy Water appears in this poem and others as the source from which the people, culture, philosophy and traditions of the Delta originate. The Delta gives and sustains life. Its waters course in and through the people themselves.

During the dance of celebration, the people are exhorted to "leaven our dance / of the Front with rhythms / of the Back and strengthen / the fragile songs of the new / with songs of mermaids." The celebration is followed by the more staid realization that independence must be followed by governance:

And the dancers disperse, walking
with feet that have known many dances
　　　. . . walking
with their hearts climbing up their feet
to their places and the palmwine descending
. . . .
　　　. . . and their faces become naked.

Okara developed his sense of language — his ear — early. Long before his own first poems were published, he devoted a considerable period to translating Ijaw lyrics into English. The incantatory tone and formal beauty of the language of "The Fisherman's Invocation" underscore not only his expertise at translating, but also his dexterity in framing the underlying cultural and philosophical constructs that drive the sequence in language shaped to his Niger Delta sensibilities and worldview. In so doing, he delivers an English that sings, chants and dances Ijaw.

In his much earlier experimental novel, Okara had employed Ijaw as the source both for dialogue and as the standard expository language of the narrative. Using Ijaw syntax, tone, diction and style throughout, the novel bypasses altogether the too common pitfalls of inscribed folk expression — characters rendered laughable, quaint or folkloric, and whose concerns are easily read as either inevitable — *The poor ye have always among ye* — and inconsequential. Okara elects to conform English to Ijaw rather than the reverse. And in so doing, he reveals the philosophical heft and lyric elegance of the Ijaw language. First published in 1964, *The Voice* was the first work of his, or any writer's, to make use of the language in this way.

The narrative traces one young man's search for a clear moral center and healing for the community to which he returns after his studies. His name, Okolo, means "the voice." And he doggedly pursues a quest for what he calls only "it."

Clearly written in response to the disillusionment experienced by many Nigerians in the first years of independence, *The Voice* is an allegory for a society that allows itself to be made complicit in the wrongdoing of a government it knows to be unethical and unjust.

> Why should Okolo look for *it*, they wondered. Things have changed, the world has turned and they are now the Elders. No one in the past has asked for *it*. Why should Okolo expect to find *it* now that they are the Elders? No, he must stop the search. He must not spoil their pleasure.
>
> So Chief Izongo spoke, at the gathering of the Elders and the Elders, in their insides, turned these spoken words over and over and looked to see the path they would take to avoid this stinking thing. They turned over the spoken words and sent messengers to Okolo to ask him to cease forthwith his search for *it*.

Okolo refuses. He publicly denounces an official gag order imposed by the elders and finds himself abandoned, one by one, by longtime friends who privately agree with him about the current state of the community, but fear the kind of ostracizing and abuse to which he is subjected. Okolo, however, will neither relent nor be silenced. His only ally is Tuere, a young woman whose name, depending on the context, means "last woman" or "last wife." Having long ago been driven out by the elders as a sorceress, she has resigned herself to a lonely and isolated existence on the very outskirts of town. Okolo, however, spurns the moral authority of the elders to banish him. The novel ends at daybreak:

> And in a canoe tied together back to back with their feet tied to the seats of the canoe, were Okolo and Tuere. Down they floated from one bank of the river to the other like debris, carried by the current. The canoe was drawn into a whirlpool. It spun round and round and was slowly drawn into the core and finally disappeared. And the water rolled over the top and the river flowed smoothly over it as if nothing had happened.

The first passage demonstrates the poetic use the author makes of Ijaw language in a book-length work of prose. The novel's concluding paragraph reveals as well the extent to which his use of conventional English prose is anchored in clear and unencumbered poetic diction.

Okara is fond of allegory, fable and myth and borrows freely from the moral and storytelling devices of these social narratives in all of the genres in which he writes: poetry, novel, short story, essay, journalism, children's books. *Lion's Dilemma: Allegorical Fable of the African Present* (2010) is the tale of a ruler unwilling and also unable to concede that his rule is not and was never meant to be absolute, that his long reign must end and a new and more just era in the history of the animal kingdom begin.

"Revolt of the Gods" is a dramatic lyric in two parts. "Argument 1," the prologue, is a brief conversation between two old and world-weary gods, apparently resigned to their role as beings of man's creation. Possessed of higher wisdom, they are nonetheless powerless to change their fate. Intimately and inextricably bound to man in an eternal cycle of birth, death and rebirth, their destiny is determined wholly by the needs and whims of their earthly creator. The list of assaults of man against the gods is appropriately interminable and exhausting:

We have died again and again
and have risen again and again
only to die again and again

in the dying whims of erratic modes
of man when man began and we
began with him countless centuries ago.

. . . .

He throws us to the mud, picks us up
refurbishes us, puts us in masks
stifling us, debases us in other guises

. . . .

as the mood catches him;
and kills us as a sacrifice to his groping mind.

"Argument 2" is a more lively debate among these older, more experienced gods who have already long known the score, and a younger god who rejects out of hand his role as "man's plaything." He attempts to rouse his elders to stand up against human caprice and claim their godly birthright. Their own argument parallels another more boisterous exchange among four men on earth below and on which the gods eavesdrop. Soon after the men begin to discuss religion, one claims to be the "Prophet of Doom! Seer of Doom!" When asked the substance of his prophecy and how the world will end, however, he stops drinking only long enough to quote scripture, replying obliquely, "Those who have ears to hear let them hear." Comic relief is offered in the form of another fellow then calling out "Hear! Hear!" He continues his drunken shouting throughout the discourse, toasting loudly, "Well spoken! Here's to you!" to the claims and charges of each speaker. Repulsed, the younger god expresses dismay and protests the crude behavior of his makers. The poem closes with an older, wiser god pointing out to him that his own voice is already fading among those of the creators below, "and thus we suffer pains of a million deaths."

In the shorter lyric poems, Okara typically presents a solitary persona intent on gaining a clearer perspective on some dilemma, spiritual, communal or having to do with the larger world. Often, the speaker confronts senseless and horrific violence, death and destruction waged against nature and humanity. Ostensibly undertaken in the name of progress, this violence and destruction are symptomatic of greed, often symbolized by "naira" — the name for Nigeria's currency. In these lines from "The Dreamer," observe how the play of assonance, near rhyme, phrasal rhythm and line in stanzas 4 and 5 plunges the reader into a dazzling maze of wanton corruption:

> Sleepless heat their nightly fare became — the marching masses;
> Worthless naira their bane became — the marching masses;
>
> Sweat soaked pariah naira made pariah by crafty shovel-hand
> Of masked greed and lurid bags and pockets in gaudy world display!
>   it roams pariah regions, valueless,
> pools of crumpled hopes in highway potholes, floating away.

The inverted phrasing of the two lines from stanza 4 introduces an atmosphere at once despondent and restless; and the regular rhythm generated by repetition of the phrase "the marching masses" creates an awareness of inevitable arrival at some awful place not yet revealed. Stanza 5 then opens with a staccato rhythm that forces the reader to sound each word separately while descending further into the scene of unabashed depravity and corruption. Followed by the too-close repetition of the slightly off-rhyme of *pariah naira pariah* and then, again *pariah*, the overall effect is that the reader is plunged breathlessly into the poem's dizzying atmosphere of "dreams turned malignant nightmare."

"The Dreamer" takes for its theme the internal difficulties engendered by government reliance since the 1980s on International Monetary Fund loans, which come with crippling austerity requirements that sink the nation into even deeper poverty. Okara plays on the irony of austerity measures named Structural Adjustment Programs, or SAP, in lines where the people's feet carry "bodies sapped by SAP to the bones / Like long trekking starving cattle with only skin hanging on bones."

Stanza 7 is the halfway point at which the Dreamer, introduced briefly at the outset as one "seeking good in our collective good," reappears as one who has "weighed, surveyed" and now joins with the "tramping stamping / Mass of feet" of the people. From this juncture, the lines evolve into a cleaner syntax, first of a series of questions — the most poignant and telling of which may be the one that asks, "Where's our common laughter kept in vaults, silos of our land?" — unfolding into stanzas made up of long reflexive single sentences before accelerating into declarative statements. Before that is fully achieved, the people progress from trekking to running as they gain strength and determination from "danger drums" that "send lightning messages": "Slowly, slowly faster and faster . . . / Blowing to flaming embers of defiance, and awakening / And massive feet of indomitable resolve." In the final stanza, the dreamer's complete union with the people is indicated by a lowercase *d*. No longer "weighing" and "surveying" the effects of full-blown corruption and conspicuous government complicity and betrayal, "now the dreamer, with machete, / Word-sharpened, is clearing the forest . . . / To sow the seed that would send its roots, / . . . to its expected greatness."

Okara's participant-observer is a man who moves easily in varied environments. Typically sophisticated, erudite, intellectually and spiritually centered, he is quiet not timid, contemplative not disengaged. Though solitary, he is not lonely. What is clear in his observations of the scene he moves in — or, as is often the case, the scene that moves about him — is that his is a worldview shaped from within a particular place and people. He neither leads nor speaks for any group, but as a member of a community. And while much of what he sees and experiences causes him to question and to suffer, he opts for a long-range view, one committed to an eventual if distant change for better. The definitive characteristic of such a speaker is that, facing loss, pain, the horrors of war, he persists.

GABRIEL OKARA

PART I

The Early Lyrics

The Call of the River Nun

I hear your call!
I hear it far away;
I hear it break the circle
of these crouching hills.

I want to view your face
again and feel your cold
embrace; or at your brim
to set myself and
inhale your breath; or
Like the trees, to watch
my mirrored self unfold
and span my days with
song from the lips of dawn.

I hear your lapping call!
I hear it coming through;
invoking the ghost of a child
listening, where river birds hail
your silver-surfaced flow.

My river's calling too!
Its ceaseless flow impels
my found'ring canoe down
its inevitable course.
And each dying year
brings near the sea-bird call,
the final call that
stills the crested waves
and breaks in two the curtain
of silence of my upturned canoe.

O incomprehensible God!
Shall my pilot be
my inborn stars to that
final call to Thee
O my river's complex course?

Once Upon a Time

Once upon a time, son,
they used to laugh with their hearts
and laugh with their eyes;
but now they only laugh with their teeth,
while their ice-block-cold eyes
search behind my shadow.

There was a time indeed
they used to shake hands with their hearts;
but that's gone, son.
Now they shake hands without hearts
while their left hands search
my empty pockets.

"Feel at home!" "Come again";
they say, and when I come
again and feel
at home, once, twice,
there will be no thrice —
for then I find doors shut on me.

So I have learned many things, son.
I have learned to wear many faces

like dresses — homeface,
officeface, streetface, hostface,
cocktailface, with all their conforming smiles
like a fixed portrait smile.

And I have learned, too,
to laugh with only my teeth
and shake hands without my heart.
I have also learned to say, "Goodbye,"
when I mean "Good-riddance";
to say "Glad to meet you,"
without being glad; and to say "It's been
nice talking to you," after being bored.

But believe me, son.
I want to be what I used to be
when I was like you. I want
to unlearn all these muting things.
Most of all, I want to relearn
how to laugh, for my laugh in the mirror
shows only my teeth like a snake's bare fangs!

So show me, son,
how to laugh; show me how
I used to laugh and smile
once upon a time when I was like you.

Piano and Drums

When at break of day at a riverside
I hear jungle drums telegraphing
the mystic rhythm, urgent, raw
like bleeding flesh, speaking of
primal youth and the beginning,
I see the panther ready to pounce,
the leopard snarling about to leap
and the hunters crouch with spears poised;

And my blood ripples, turns torrent,
topples the years and at once I'm
in my mother's lap a suckling;
at once I'm walking simple
paths with no innovations,
rugged, fashioned with the naked
warmth of hurrying feet and groping hearts
in green leaves and wild flowers pulsing.

Then I hear a wailing piano
solo speaking of complex ways
in tear-furrowed concerto;
of far-away lands
and new horizons with
coaxing diminuendo, counterpoint,
crescendo. But lost in the labyrinth
of its complexities, it ends in the middle
of a phrase at a daggerpoint.

And I lost in the morning mist
of an age at a riverside keep
wandering in the mystic rhythm
of jungle drums and the concerto.

Were I to Choose

When Adam broke the stone
and red streams raged down to
gather in the womb,
an angel calmed the storm;

And, I, the breath mewed
in Cain, unblinking gaze
at the world without
from the brink of an age

That draws from the groping lips
a breast-muted cry
to thread the years.
(O were I to choose)

And now the close of one
and thirty turns, the world
of bones is Babel, and
the different tongues within
are flames the head
continually burning.

And O of this dark halo
were the tired head free.

And when the harmattan
of days has parched the throat
and skin, and sucked the fever
of the head away,

Then the massive dark
descends, and flesh and bone
are razed. And (O were I to choose) I'd cheat the worms
and silence seek in stone.

Spirit of the Wind

The storks are coming now—
white specks in the silent sky.
They had gone north seeking
fairer climes to build their homes
when here was raining.

They are back with me now—
Spirits of the wind,
beyond the god's confining
hands they go north and west and east,
instinct guiding.

But willed by the gods
I'm sitting on this rock
watching them come and go
from sunrise to sundown, with the spirit
urging within.

And urging a red pool stirs,
and each ripple is
the instinct's vital call,
a desire in a million cells
confined.

O God of the gods and me,
shall I not heed
this prayer-bell call, the noon
angelus, because my stork is caged
in Singed Hair and Dark Skin?

New Year's Eve Midnight

Now the bells are tolling—
A year is dead.
And my heart is slowly beating
the Nunc Dimittis
to all my hopes and mute
yearnings of a year
and ghosts hover round
dream beyond dream

Dream beyond dream
mingling with the dying
bell-sounds fading
into memories
like rain drops
falling into a river.

And now the bells are chiming—
A year is born.
And my heart-bell is ringing
in a dawn.
But it's shrouded things I see
dimly stride
on heart-canopied paths
to a riverside.

You Laughed and Laughed and Laughed

In your ears my song
is motor car misfiring
stopping with a choking cough;
and you laughed and laughed and laughed.

In your eyes my ante-
natal walk was inhuman, passing
your "omnivorous understanding"
and you laughed and laughed and laughed.

You laughed at my song,
you laughed at my walk.

Then I danced my magic dance
to the rhythm of talking drums pleading, but you shut your
eyes and laughed and laughed and laughed.

And then I opened my mystic
inside wide like
the sky, instead you entered your
car and laughed and laughed and laughed.

You laughed at my dance,
you laughed at my inside.

You laughed and laughed and laughed.
But your laughter was ice-block
laughter and it froze your inside froze
your voice froze your ears
froze your eyes and froze your tongue.

And now it's my turn to laugh;
but my laughter is not
ice-block laughter. For I
know not cars, know not ice-blocks.

My laughter is the fire
of the eye of the sky, the fire
of the earth, the fire of the air,
the fire of the seas and the
rivers fishes animals trees
and it thawed your inside,
thawed your voice, thawed your
ears, thawed your eyes and
thawed your tongue.

So a meek wonder held
your shadow and you whispered:
"Why so?"
And I answered:
"Because my fathers and I
are owned by the living
warmth of the earth
through our naked feet."

The Mystic Drum

The mystic drum beat in my inside
and fishes danced in the rivers
and men and women danced on land
to the rhythm of my drum

But standing behind a tree
with leaves around her waist
she only smiled with a shake of her head.

Still my drum continued to beat,
rippling the air with quickened
tempo compelling the quick
and the dead to dance and sing
with their shadows—

But standing behind a tree
with leaves around her waist
she only smiled with a shake of her head.

Then the drum beat with the rhythm
of the things of the ground
and invoked the eye of the sky
the sun and the moon and the river gods—
and the trees began to dance,
the fishes turned men
and men turned fishes
and things stopped to grow—

But standing behind a tree
with leaves around her waist
she only smiled with a shake of her head.

And then the mystic drum
in my inside stopped to beat —
and men became men,
fishes became fishes
and trees, the sun and the moon
found their places, and the dead
went to the ground and things began to grow.

And behind the tree she stood
with roots sprouting from her
feet and leaves growing on her head
and smoke issuing from her nose
and her lips parted in her smile
turned cavity belching darkness.

Then, then I packed my mystic drum
and turned away; never to beat so loud any more.

One Night at Victoria Beach

The wind comes rushing from the sea,
the waves curling like mambas strike
the sands and recoiling hiss in rage
washing the Aladuras' feet pressing hard
on the sand and with eyes fixed hard
on what only hearts can see, they shouting
pray, the Aladuras pray; and coming
from booths behind, compelling highlife
forces ears; and car lights startle pairs
arm in arm passing washer-words back
and forth like haggling sellers and buyers —

Still they pray, the Aladuras pray
with hands pressed against their hearts
and their white robes pressed against
their bodies by the wind; and drinking
palmwine and beer, the people boast
at bars at the beach. Still they pray.

They pray, the Aladuras pray
to what only hearts can see while dead
fishermen long dead with bones rolling
nibbled clean by nibbling fishes, follow
four dead cowries shining like stars
into deep sea where fishes sit in judgement;
and living fishermen in dark huts
sit round dim lights with Babalawo
throwing their souls in four cowries
on sand, trying to see tomorrow.

Still they pray, the Aladuras pray
to what only hearts can see behind
the curling waves and the sea, the stars
and the subduing unanimity of the sky
and their white bones beneath the sand.

And standing dead on dead sands,
I felt my knees touch living sands —
but the rushing wind killed the budding words.

The Snowflakes Sail Gently Down

The snowflakes sail gently
down from the misty eye of the sky
and fall lightly on the
winter-weary elms. And the branches
winter-stripped and nude, slowly
with the weight of the weightless snow
bow like grief-stricken mourners
as white funeral cloth is slowly
unrolled over deathless earth.
And dead sleep stealthily from the
heater rose and closed my eyes with
the touch of silk cotton on water falling.

Then I dreamed a dream
in my dead sleep. But I dreamed
not of earth dying and elms a vigil
keeping. I dreamed of birds, black
birds flying in my inside, nesting
and hatching on oil palms bearing suns
for fruits and with roots denting the
uprooters' spades. And I dreamed the
uprooters tired and limp, leaning on my roots —
their abandoned roots
and the oil palms gave them each a sun.

But on their palms
they balanced the blinding orbs
and frowned with schisms on their
brows — for the suns reached not
the brightness of gold!

Then I awoke. I awoke
to the silently falling snow
and bent-backed elms bowing and
swaying to the winter wind like
white-robed Moslems salaaming at evening
prayer, and the earth lying inscrutable
like the face of a god in a shrine.

Adhiambo

I hear many voices
like it's said a madman hears;
I hear trees talking
like it's said a medicine man hears.

Maybe I'm a madman
I'm a medicine man.
Maybe I'm mad,
for the voices are luring me,
urging me from the midnight
moon and the silence of my desk
to walk on wave crests across a sea.

Maybe I'm a medicine man
hearing talking saps,
seeing behind trees;
but who's lost his powers
of invocation.

But the voices and the trees
are now a name-spelling and one figure

silence-etched across
the moonface is walking, stepping
over continents and seas.

And I raised my hand —
my trembling hand, gripping
my heart as handkerchief
and waved and waved and waved
but she turned her eyes away.

To Paveba

When young fingers stir
the fire smoldering in my inside
the dead weight of dead years rolls
crashing to the ground
and the fire begins to flame anew,

The fire begins to flame anew
devouring the debris of years —
the dry harmattan-sucked trees,
the dry tearless faces
smiling weightless smiles like breath
that do not touch the ground.

The fire begins to flame anew
and I laugh and shout to the eye
of the sky on the back of a fish
and I stand on the wayside
smiling the smile of budding trees
at men and women whose insides

are filled with ashes, who
tell me, "We once had our flaming fire."

Then I remember my vow.
I remember my vow not to let
my fire flame any more. And the dead
years rise creaking from the ground
and file slowly into my inside
and shyly push aside the young fingers
and smother the devouring flame.

And as before the fire smolders in water,
continually smoldering beneath
the ashes with things I dare not tell
erupting from the hackneyed lore
of the beginning. For they die in the telling.

So let them be. Let them smolder.
Let them smolder in the living fire beneath the ashes.

"Franvenkirche"

(Our Lady's Cathedral, Munich)

I am standing on an age which is now
an object of curiosity and wonder
and which has withstood centuries
and perfected means of destruction.

I am indeed standing on Faith
absolute Faith, twin-towered Faith

in which echoes of whispered prayers
clinging to the walls give one a feeling
strange yet not strange. A feeling
which knows no language no creed
and running through my inside
to my hands made them one
with those that set brick upon brick
to build this memorial, this symbol of Faith
and landmark to this city of Munich

Munich, 1963

Fantasy

A cloud as dark as darkest night,
Immense as a looming mountain,
Slowly descends on a sunny day;
And men and women in abject dismay
Shut their eyes and raise their hands in protest!

But the cloud slowly descends
And gives prophetic tongues to birds and leaves
And blades of grass and yam and cassava shoots
And goats and sheep!

And men and women listen, abdicating
Their dominion to seek mediators
In sacrificial eggs and a babel of tongues!

Still the silent cloud descends,
Slipping into hearts and minds
And men and women become docile cattle
Being led to the slaughter house.

The Passing of a Year

I have killed the year
That has killed me
And I have killed love
That is not is —

Goodbye dying year
Goodbye love

Goodbye nameless things
That have cracked the walls
Of my inside with hammer
Blows that stoppered my ears
And held fast my eyes

Goodbye all

Goodbye Gecko, spirit
Of the house that sheltered
Me with your mystery
Strolling down walls,
For now I must go and face
Faceless things, brutal things,
Savaging my inside.

And goodbye the head
That killed my malaria
Fever coursing in my veins
And sensitive fingers
That tended yam shoots and birth
Is no more time for palm wine
So I have killed the year
That has killed me and shake
The new with hands that again

Will do it in, and I have killed
Love that never is.

And so goodbye dying year
And goodbye faceless things
Goodbye Gecko
With your mystery
Stamped on ceilings and walls —

Goodbye potent head
That defies my head!

And goodbye fingers
That once felt the flow
Of sap and were tickled by yam shoots

And goodbye my weeping senses —
Goodbye, goodbye all, goodbye!

1960–62

The Gambler

I opened my palm wide,
my fingers pointing into five directions,
then I placed the dice
on the geometrical center
and closed my palm with prayers
from five directions invoking
CHANCE for SIX!

Then I brought it near to my lips
and gave it teaching words;
I brought it near my lips
and blew my breath on it;
I brought it near my lips
and prayed to LUCK for SIX!

Then with my sweating shadow
and my trembling inside dripping
with emotions, I shook the dice
over my head seven times and shutting
my eyes let it drop from my palm!

I slowly opened my eyes
and saw the dice suspended
between earth and sky, dancing,
before my eyes and a hand reached
down from the sky and snatched it away!

1963

PART II

The Fisherman's Invocation

1

Introit

Cast your net to the rightside
Nothing?
   Nothing

Cast it to the leftside
Nothing?
   Nothing

Then cast it to the back of the canoe
and draw gently and carefully
while I paddle the canoe forward —
Nothing?

   It's only the Back caught
   in the meshes of Today
   and I see past moons past suns
   past nights and past gods reflected
   by the Back trying to slip
   through the Meshes like a fish

Draw gently
draw carefully
don't let it slip
draw it up into
the canoe and let's hold
it in our palms
the Back, the gods,
even for only
one still moment

one still moment
one teaching moment

    My hands tremble
    for I fear the masquerades
    of the resurrecting Back

Draw man draw
Strengthen your Chest
The Front grows from the Back
like buds from a tree stump

    Do buds sprout from dead stumps?
    The stump of my Back is standing dead
    in a desert and its essence
    is with the desert sun

Your back's stump is not dead.
Deep down in the desert
there's water bubbling up to your roots
So draw, draw the Back
caught in the net into the canoe
and stretch forth your hands
into the face of the sun
and pluck down the essence
of the stump of your Back

    In the face of the sun
    I see only darkness
    At the back of my Back
    I see only darkness
    and the water in the desert
    has dried in darkness

No darkness no light
no light no darkness
You are seeing chicken
giving birth to a lamb
There's water at the back
of your Back gushing from a womb

    There's no more substance
    from a womb. The water
    dried up after the flood
    showing skeletons and dead wood

Dig deep at the back
of the womb. There's water
there's water from a river
flowing from the bottom of the Back
of the womb. So draw up the Back caught
in the net. Draw it up and let's look it over
in our insides, in our heads

    The Back is my first
    little paddle I lost
    in the river and whose
    shape I cannot now remember

Then let your head
be the head of an elephant
let your eyes be the eyes
of a leopard and stalk the Back
stalk the Back in the forest
stalk the Back in the heavens
stalk it in the earth
stalk it in your umbilical cord.

Look behind trees look behind
moon fleeing from angry sun
look behind sun with flaming
eyes lashed fixed by broom of moon
and stalk it behind burnt
teeth of Cricket burnt from laughing
at Earth in water dissolving

    I cannot turn my eyes
    for I am caught in grim
    teeth of trap of Today

Then the Front is dying
in the womb of the river
and on your laps will lie
a still-birth Front
and you'll no more go
to the ponds to fish
you'll no more throw
your net in the river
With your dead Back
hanging on your back
and your dead Front
lying on your laps
You'll no more be man among
men; for you have defiled the Back
and the Things of the ground
and have killed the gods of the Back
So let go the Back in the net
Let your weeping gods drop
into the river and come to the prow
and I will to the bow
and I will catch the Back
and the weeping Gods in the net

and give them power
to thrust my hand into the face of the sun
as the moon with a broom and pluck down
the Essence of your dead stump
and bring forth the Child-Front.

2

The Invocation

See the sun in my hands
    I see
See the Gods in the sun
    I see
See the Back in my hands
    I see
See the Front in my hands
    I see

You are seeing the sun in my hands
You are seeing Gods in my hands
You are seeing the Back in my hands
You are seeing the Front in my hands

    I see
    I see

See the moon in my hands
    I see

You are seeing the moon in my hands
You are seeing the back of the womb

    I see
    I see

You are just a shape in the womb
The living shape of your Back
The living shape of the Earth

    I am
    I am
    I am just a shape in the womb
    I am just a shape of my Back
    I am just a shape of the Earth

You are just a shape of the Earth
The Earth is the womb of wombs
The sun is sperm of sperms
and the sun is playing in your front

    the sun is playing in my front
    urging my blood to the Back
    and the Front; the sun is playing
    in my front and I hear the song
    of the Back coming rushing
    rushing coming. I am wrapped
    in steps of the dancing Back
    and I can hear, I can hear the Front
    coming gently coming painfully coming

O midwifemoon rub gently down
the back of your Back
while the sun plays his play

and the Back dance its dance
and assembly of mermaids
sing their bubbling water song
beneath the river waves

O play, let the sun play
and rub rub midwifemoon
down the back of the Back.
For the Front is coming gushing
coming with sound of river
rushing over a fall subduing
barriers of height and stone

And let O let the deep drums
of deep water boom and mingle
with deep drums of deep Gods
in their play in your inside
Let them mingle O mingle with the clatter
of the drums of Today
for the coming, safe coming of the Front

The Front is coming
breaking through my
ruptured inside.
The Front is coming
but its lightning
a million-tongued lightning
flashing, exploding in my head

Rumble thunder God rumble.
Stride down to the edge
of the world and rumble
until your booming voice
encircles the earth

booming until the earth
trembles in agony of birth

    The Front is coming
    It is a ball of fire
    searing through my being
    and I tremble at the full birth-course.
    The earth trembles and I am wrapped
    in lightning wail-song of the Front.

Stretch forth your hands
O striding Gods and temper
O temper the fireball Front
with your mystic touch. And let
O let it rest in your teaching hands
and mold it with the mold
of the back of the womb.

3

The Child-Front

The child-Front has come
    What child is it?
It came with the head
    What is it?
It came without teeth
    Did it come talking?
Wait, let it take form
The sun-play is not ended
    Did it not cry?
It is not yet human

Where are your Gods now
Gods of the Back that have
brought forth this monster?
Throw it away, throw it into
the river and let the mermaids
carry it on their songs.
Throw it away to the Back
and let the Back swallow it in its abyss
And let the Gods remember their lives are in my hands

Patience man patience
The play is not ended
and midwifemoon with it in her hands
is rising on the crest of darkness
to the eye of the sky

I want to hear no more of midwifemoon
I want to hear no more of the back of the womb

Patience I say patience
and the spent sun is slowly climbing
climbing down a burning ladder
to regain his powers, his force
beneath smoky roofs

So do not reject the Back
and abandon your child-Front
before the sun ends his play
the Back its molding dance
the mermaids their water song
and midwifemoon her rise

Sleep with a sweet inside and dream
for the sun will rise singing

and midwifemoon will come down smiling
and deliver into your hands in your dream
a child a human child that will not burn your hands.

So let's fish no more.
Steer the canoe to our hearths
and let's warm ourselves
with the songs of the Back and songs
of the coming Front entwined
like tendrils in our inside
to await the coming of midwifemoon

4

Birth Dance of the Child-Front

Let's dance with feet
that yesterday knows
and sing with voice
that breaks into tomorrow

Let's dance let's sing
Let's sing and dance
for the great child-Front
has come is coming

Let's drink and dance
let palm wine flow
like the Niger flow
and raise our feet
and shake the ground

Let's dance let's sing
Let's sing and dance
for the great child-Front
has come is coming

Let your feet be
knowing-something feet
and let your voice be
knowing-something voice

Let's dance let's sing
let's sing and dance
for the great child-Front
has come is coming

Let's dance with rhythms
of things of the Front
Raise the dead with song and dance
raze to the ground all thwarting things.

Let's dance let's sing
let's sing and dance
for the great child-Front
has come is coming

Let's leaven our dance
of the Front with rhythms
of the Back and strengthen
the fragile songs of the new
with songs of mermaids

So roll your eyes
and sway your hips
to the Back and Front

Raise your voice
to the eye of the sky
with songs that are tall and strong

    Let's dance let's sing
    Let's sing and dance
    for the great child-Front
    has come is coming

Now song and wine
are up in our heads
and voice up in the sky
burning the sun and the moon

And so the rhythm has changed
but not the theme —
Dance in circles
sing in circles
stamp your feet
to the circular drums

    Dance in circles
    in endless dance
    sing in circles
    no beginning no end

No beginning no end
we dance and dance
to coming Fronts
to passing Fronts
without beginning without end

So dance dance
change your steps

change your songs
tie your steps
tie your songs
to the changing beat
till song and dance
and beat of drum
join in one to keep
from mischief the great child-Front

    Let's sing and dance
    in endless circles
    till song and dance
    and beat of drum join in one

Dance dance
your muscles tremble
your fingers tingle
with the spirit of the dance
and the spirit of the Front

    Let's dance let's sing
    let's sing and dance
    for the great child-Front
    has come is coming

5

The End

The celebration is now ended
but the echoes are all around
whirling like a harmattan
whirlwind throwing dust around
and hands cover faces and feet grope

The celebration is now ended
the drums lie quiet, silent, waiting.
And the dancers disperse, walking
with feet that have known many dances
waiting for the next; walking
with their hearts climbing up their feet
to their places and the palmwine descending
from their heads to settle in their bellies
and their bodies turn cold. For the spirit
of the dance has left and their faces become naked.

But the child-Front is now lying on laps
feeding from measureless breasts of the Back
Singing green lullabies which tingle our heads.
And we learn to sing half familiar half strange songs
We learn to dance to half familiar half strange
rhythms fashioned in dreams as the child-Front
Lay sleeping with breasts in his mouth.

PART III

War Poems

Moods from Songs without Words

(1)

Sitting here on an un-cushioned chair
And Enugu lying in slumber like a tired
Coal miner, I am in a stupor, drugged
By light-blue notes of music dropping
Elegantly out of silence, and my feverish
Emotions, rising and falling with each note,
Surround me with impatient images seeking
To be born. Some are weeping, some are
Seducing me with gaiety and some just stare at
Me like Poku my cat, trying to communicate
By rubbing their sides against my emotions.

But with the last note dying into silence,
I am turned gray, cheeks sunken, face lined
Eyeglasses on nose, and with thin legs stretched
Out on the foot-rest of camp-chair, I watch.
At a riverside, a tree stump, swaying in the
Current, slowly sink into the river.

Then a lady of no known hue, with her features
Hidden behind my emotions, beckons diffidently,
And rising, I adjust my loin cloth, and walk
Shakily into the shade of a house for my
Last cup of tea.

(11)

I am just a shadow
Cast hither and thither
By rising sun and setting sun
And when the sun stands on my head
I am no more
So think of me as a shadow
Flitting from extreme to extreme.

Leave Us Alone

Though our women children born unborn
Done to death by inhuman hands
Bespattered with blood of praying men
In rooms and worshipping in church
And chapel are crying for human vengeance,
There's no vengeance in our heart.

    Leave us alone

Leave us also in our home, our land
To heal our wounds and tend orphans
Widows the maimed and let time erase
Your blind hate and reveal
To you the terrible deed of your hands;
But this, you say will not be
For, in the silence of the aftermath,
You dared not face the thirty-thousand cries, the cries
Of the children you did to death in your madness!

And so like one who drinks, drinks, and drinks
To deaden truth he cannot face,
You brushed aside pleading sanity
With hands red with blood to still kill
And plunder in our homes, in our land
To mute pleas of your conscience.
Yet this deed, this war you wage, you say
Is in the name of unity
What unity, what unity
Is it that you've so defiled, profaned?

Or unity with our bones in crossless graves?
No! not when virile blood still flows
In our veins. And so we've dealt out blows for blow
And violent deaths for death of each of our kin.

And now you feel chilling hands of death
Creeping slowly, but steadily,
Up your spine of clay. Now you hear weeping, moaning and wailing.
But this has no remorse brought to your heart.
It instead has increased your craze
And you scour the world with sedative falsehood
For accomplices in your hideous crimes, crimes
Which have numbed the conscience of even those
We admired most into impotence and shameless servitude.

But falsehood never endures, never
Stands immortal truth. There lies our strength,
Though we fight alone as those who've fought
Before for freedom which burned and ever
Will burn in the yearning hearts of those deprived
Of this sacred right. And we will surely win

As those before had won. It's Heaven's
Divine design in creation; it's a law sublime.
Know therefore, you who the world suborned,

Know you that your venture is one
You cannot sustain even with your
Borrowed men and arms by palsied
Conscience lent, and notwithstanding your daily
Illusions of victory
Victory illusory as rainbow bridge.
It's beyond your reach as water was to Tantalus.

So stop this war, this unholy war
Which serves naught but vanity,
Your consuming vanity, vanity
That battens on fresh blood of youth
You send to death by our reluctant hands;
Youth we knew by name and loved as kins.
Each such youth that dies is a bloody shroud
You are winding round your bewildered self,
You will be your own assassin

We have no vengeance, no hatred, in our hearts,
Though you harried us out of land we built and loved.
All we ask now is leave us alone in our home.

But if this war you do not cease.
A war which has the sanctity of
Truth defiled and with vanity
You soar high with soldered wings,
Closing your ears to sanity's plaintive call,
O modern Icarus!
By the sun, the Rising Sun of Biafra
You will, like your mentor, come to ignominious fall!

Leave us alone in our Fatherland
Leave us alone to built the land —
The land of our dreams, and of freedom,
Justice, Hope, Opportunity —
Where no one will ever be oppressed, suborned;
Leave us alone to build our homes
And raise our families in peace and plenty
Leave us alone

That's all we ask of you and of the world.

December 1967

I Am Only a Name

I am only a name
a name in the air
intruding into your peace
like an unpleasant noise
and not of flesh and blood —
flesh and blood clinging
to your bones and running
in your veins.

I am only an episode
in the morning papers
which you put aside
or throw into wastepaper baskets
and turn to your bacon and egg
and milk for your young
while I whom you have

drained of flesh and blood
tread with bare feet on thorns
in bushes searching, searching
for tiny snails and insects
for my young with swollen feet.

I am only a name
an expendable name
not of the human folds
and while collapsing children
gasp their last breath
by waysides and mothers'
saltless tears form streams
on my face; and while
I am drenched with stench
of blood and rotting flesh

I am only expendable name
thrown back and forth
in ritual jokes in corridors
of sacrificial shrines
and not for your ears
for that would break the spell
which makes me only a name
as we stagger, my young and I
with nothing between skin and bone
into the gathering darkness.

Yet my heart sings of the day,
the day bursting with song
and the smile of my young
yes, my heart sings in this darkness
of the moaning, dying
dying because the spell

makes me only a name
an expendable name.

Yet my heart sings
as I weakly genuflect
to the calling Angelus bells
which reach out to me like
hands out of the gathering darkness

The Silent Voice

The moon's rays whispering low and soft
Like a mother calming her child in nightmare,
Shed troubled heart and mind of yesterday's fears
In the mystery of sleep as the hours, hand
Over hand draw near tomorrow's dawn.
And as I stand listening in the moon
And the silence of the street, I hear
Scurrying feet of fear muffled by the moon
And the youthful laugh of hope ringing from dawn
Though tomorrow each hour will be moving hour of lips
In prayer like fingers groping over Rosary beads,
Counting hours for nightfall and moon fall —
And when shadows darken and the day passes
As yesterday with its dead into memory of the living
I wait with bated breath for the moon's whispers. . . .

I wait for the moon's whispers
From heaven's beneficence to rehabilitate
Limbs, mind, and heart and turn the spirit
Of liberty skywards to face planes at dawn.

Planes spitting bombs and bullets at Truth —
Leaving mangled bones and homes (a mission completed)!
Then silver-winged death fearing death flies away
In white-speckled blue sky, darting from cloud to cloud
As defiant guns and deathless spirits
Reach behind the clouds to pluck it down in anger —
But it flies away, and tearless eyes turn downwards
To carry limbs, heads, limbless headless bodies
In solemn silence to nameless graves. . . .
And when shadows darken and the day passes
As yesterday with its dead into memory of the living
I wait with bated breath for the moon's whispers. . . .

I wait for the moon's whispers
From above like the ailing for the healer;
I listen continually with my heart for the whisper
Which comes from beyond the moon too gentle for the ear
To restore to bleeding will and gasping hope
Yesterday's strength and to staunch inward wounds
Daytime wounds of alienating words and deeds
Of the living, I listen continually —
I listen to the silent voice from whence comes
The whisper like morning breeze from river unseen,
To lean my battered hopes battered by battles within
And wait for night in labor to bear forth the birth cry at dawn
And dedication to derivations of peace in honor
Of our maimed, our dead, and for posterity. . . .

Suddenly the Air Cracks

Suddenly the air cracks
with striking cracking rockets
guffaw of bofors stuttering LMGs
jets diving shooting glasses dropping
breaking from lips people diving
under beds nothing bullets flashing fire
striking writhing bodies and walls —

Suddenly there's silence —
And a thick black smoke
rises sadly into the sky as the jets
fly away in gruesome glee —

Then a babel of emotions, voices
mothers fathers calling children
and others joking shouting "where's your bunker?"
laughing teasing across streets
and then they gaze in groups without sadness
at the sad smoke curling skywards —

Again suddenly, the air cracks
above rooftops cracking striking
rockets guffawing bofors stuttering LMGs
ack ack flacks diving jets
diving men women dragging children
seeking shelter not there breathless
hugging gutters walls houses
crumbling rumbling thunder
bombs hearts thumping heads low
under beds moving wordless lips —

Then suddenly there's silence —
and the town heaves a deep sigh
as the jets again fly away and the guns
one by one fall silent and the gunners
dazed gaze at the empty sky, helpless —

And then voices shouting calling
voices, admiring jet's dive
pilots' bravery blaming gunners
praising gunners laughing people
wiping sweat and dust from hair
neck and shirt with trembling hands.
Things soon simmer to normal
hum and rhythm as danger passes
and the streets are peopled
with strolling men and women
boys and girls on various errands
walking talking laughing smiling —
and children running with arms
stretched out in front playing
at diving jets zoom past
unsmiling bombing rocketing shooting
with mouths between startled feet.

This also passes as dusk descends
and a friendly crescent moon
appears where the jets were.
Then simmering silence — the day passes —
And the curling black smoke,
the sadless hearts and the mangled
bodies stacked in the morgue
become memorials of this day.

Metaphor of a War

There she sat
In the dust of a field,
Head drooping like limp leaves,
And lifts a little stone
With little fingers,
Skin shrunken to the bones,
To break a palm fruit nut
To stay malignant hunger
While others of her kind
A short distance away, weakly
Played but with not a smile,
Not a sound, from sagging lips
As they tottered ungainly
With the weight of their heads
And swollen stomachs —
Sound was dead in a field of children!

Then suddenly — screams!
Screams clinging to bursting
Rockets and bombs
As MIGs whistled gaily away
Cutting a path of death — gloating death!

But there she still sat —
Shaken only by spasms
Of a whimper, as two broken
Streams of tears rolled
On to her distended stomach
As she slowly rolled on her side
Over the widening pool
Of her blood and her tears,
With not a sound as if in quiet sleep —

Cancerous Growth

The noon sun
shrivels tender buds
today's wanton massacre
burns up tender words
and from the ashes
hate is growing, forcing its way
like mushroom through yielding soil
But it's an alien growth
a cancer that destroys its host.

Umuahia, 13 December 1968

Freedom Day

It is twenty years ago today
it's twenty years ago, they said
the gods with their godly wands
broke the chains that manacled
man to man's ideologies
and so broke man's hold on man
It's twenty years ago

But look wherever you will —
North, South, East and West of the globe
look wherever you will
the same gods like hogs are shoving
squealing each other deaf
with snouts deep in blood

seeking happiness, sustenance
from Man's plaintive stream
of cries, cries tugging at the chains
broken twenty years ago.

Umuahia, 1968

Moon in the Bucket

Look!
Look out there
in the bucket
the rusty bucket
with water unclean

Look!
A luminous plate is floating—
the Moon, dancing to the gentle night wind
Look! all you who shout across the wall
with a million hates. Look at the dancing moon
It is peace unsoiled by the murk
and dirt of this bucket war.

Flying over the Sahara

1

Sand, sand, only dry sand
and scraggy rocks like
leprous fingers clawing at the plane
for a hold to pluck it down.
Here all is dead
Even the wind is dead
or ought to be dead.
But the immortal mind
with its nimble fingers
has weaned from the bowels
of the earth oil in flames
and dark smoke curling
upwards fuels his mind
and machines to build
and destroy, to nurture life and kill.

2

Dry rocks below rocking plane
with skeletons of water that were
winding between gorges like groping
mind in eternal search for fulfillment.
For how long this search only the waters
know, sucked away by craving sands
and only the weary dead know
consumed by implacable time.

Kindly Sprite

Gently mold of my mold
Hovering in a ray of light;
Kindly spirited Sprite
Dances out of pleading hold!

Fly not away, O Sprite!
I'll not bruise your lips of rose
With lacquered pose
not bedim your wings of light!

Come clinging tendrils close
And whisper tales yet untold
Of your heart's ventures old
I will mine, in sweet repose.

Gentle mold of my mold
Do not fail my feeble sight
For in the darkest night
My fingers will grope for loving hold.

18 June 1968

Rural Path

Tunnel of dreams, dreaming tunnel
of powdery sand, soft to footfall, moonfall
filtering through windless air and silent leaves —
this green peace of rural path through green walls of moss
silences bludgeoning fears and nagging primal instinct.
For soft sand and night sounds — this path
of light and shadow smother harshness of a whimsical day.

Yet this night of peace in light and darkness
with these sounds and fireflies, winking like stars
in the bushes; this night will run its course
and tomorrow will pronounce idiom of war and death
mingled with mating calls of mating birds at dawn
to efface this abbreviated peace in dreaming
tunnel dappled with light and shadow dripping
from leaves, silent drooping leaves in moondrenched dreams.

Ogwa, 1969

Lady and Her Wig

She talked of Paris
Abidjan, Gabon, Lisbon —
This lady of the black wig,
With the latest in shoes and gown!

  "You are well turned out, lady."
  "Thank you," she said and then

"The wig is from Paris."
    I said yes.
"The shoes from Gabon."
"The dress from Lisbon."
    I said yes.
"You are not looking!" she screamed,
Seeing my eyes turned elsewhere at thighs,
A boy's thighs with skin hanging
And hands dangling palsied by Kwashiorkor
Slowly lifting his swollen feet
To move a step, by a painful, weary step,
Into a path in the forest!

Ogwa, 1969

Silent Girl

Sweet silent girl
what makes you speak not
what makes you speak not
of our days, and the days before?
what makes you speak not but only in silence
with your lips tight and tongue pressed against
your teeth by your pressing thoughts?
Is it because of the sneering, nagging present?
the present that has scotched yams, corn and minds,
the present that has turned babies to adults
and adults to babies, babbling babies
learning how to crawl and walk —
the present that has turned night sounds
of rural peace to sounds of exploding shells
and rattling guns and raucous laughter of death

and days of promise to heavy heart-crushing days;
The present that has dried us all of emotion
and the youth of youth like harmattan the trees of living sap.
Let's break with the past that bred the present
and let today be reminder of tomorrow
though tomorrow may only be a dream
as dream may vanish in our waking
or may survive — you, the silent one, or me who sings.
So be silent sweet girl
I'll be silent, speak in silence,
and let's recline on tomorrow of our dream
in the shadows of our silent thoughts
away from the hot sneering days.

Ogwa, 1969

Cross on the Moon

It is a moonlit night
the trees droop with leaves
heavy with cooling dew
gently reflect the moon descending
on soft hedges where comes forth
the screech of gleeful crickets
and the winking fire of fireflies.
Above, the plane circling, waits its turn
humming down hope into hearts
as it crosses again and again the circle of moon
then suddenly it stopped, it remained still —
it turned a cross on the moon
A testimony of Man's humanity breaking its bonds

and sallying forth into dangers known and unknown
to spread succor to those in their last sleep
and whose hopes have dried in parched
throats and whimpering children
on backs of fearless mothers.

Ogwa, 1969

Rain Lullaby

Soothe me not to sleep gentle rain
with your lullaby on eager
yam and cassava leaves and on
pan roof drumming beats of love
For now is not time for sleep or love
or tender emotions of days gone by
When the earth, sun and moon
juggled night and day in my head
which now is home for vampires
and silent bats flitting from wall
to wall preying on my essence
Now is time to record wickedness
bursting far and near by day
and the hum and rhythm of bravery in mercy
high in the sky at night dropping
milk in drops into open mouths
open like baby birds waiting
for feed from mother birds.

Come, Come and Listen

Come sit with me awhile
away from your golden crowns,
pause awhile from poking the fire
beneath the burning funeral pyre
and listen to the song beyond the flames
set by trembling hands to drown my cry.
Come, sit with me you who proudly fly
beyond the heaven on eagle's wings —
Listen to flame-song beyond the flames.

Come, O come, with me awhile
you who built my pyre with hasty hands
and listen to the song gurgling through
molten lead poured down my throat
song sung with tongues of impatient flames
threading me like beads round the neck
of struggling centuries. Come, come and listen!

Come and listen to whimpered songs
of charred stumps of promise tied to mothers' backs
trembling, rooted to the ground in pouring rain —
waiting, waiting with hands raised skywards
to mercy buzzing in serene clouds.

Come, sit with me you who proudly fly
beyond the heavens on eagle's wings —
Listen to whimpered song beyond flames.
Seeking not seeking the end
of tremulous hopes men stopper ears
to strident slogans and take refuge
in primal instinct move eyes to occiputs

to see vista back to wombs, but unreceptive,
indignant wombs. So they turn back, evading
eyes of children, unopen leaves of a tendril dying.
Come with me and listen
to the rattle of dying tendrils.

O come with me awhile
you who drew triggers with tongues
up in the clouds, traversing continents and seas
and taught self-emasculation as propitiation
of your aspiring godship of the universe,
come and drink the hot song of blood
served up on green cocoyam leaves which knew
once only globes of cooling dew
Come, come and drink with the wafer
of my hopes and savor your deeds!
I will rise wise and seek mercy from the eyes
of shriveled innocence, asking questions I cannot
now answer

Ogwa, 1969

Sunday

Shards of broken rays
through palm fronds
from rising sun face
hidden behind purple clouds;
birds' songs piercing the morning
babel of sounds of cars and voices
Babies' and hawkers' cries

and unspoken words and smiles
stamped on lips and wishes
masking reality of the day
I wake with half-dead prayers
falling limply out of my lips
to the belated watchman striking the hour.

I wake with half-dead prayers
with blinking eyes gauging
the sharpness of the shards of light
through sharp-edged blades of louvres
groan with lost dreams lost
in fading darkness and approaching
light with light steps silent
walking on still stream

Then church bells chime prayer hour
And the preacher with stern and solemn
mien steps on lectern to address
the faithful men and women in Sunday dress
of gold damask lace and silk
smoothing folds and creases
straightening ties and collars, freeze
the word on the preacher's lips.

Dispensing Morning Balm

Dispensing morning balm
in crystal drops of songs
into the yawning city
and the rumble and asthmatic
whizzing of a young day,
these birds erase dreams
and nightmares of the fading darkness.

To a Star

I

I strain my tired voice in song
to reach up to the star by the moon
a song I vowed never more to sing;
But from sundown to sunrise
I seek a union continually
which breaks my vow and I sing
a silent song to the rhythm of aging drums
drums not heeding constraints of fear
Bear the song tenderly toward an ear

But enfeebled by layers of falling years
the muted song reaches not the star

Still with a beggar's persistence I sing
vainly seeking harmony with song and drum
drum waxing louder, fed by each passing day

But it echoes only in the hills of dead years
and reaches not the STAR by the moon

Yet I dare to hope for a confluence of songs
    Mine enfeebled, sluggish
    The STAR's bright, engulfing
This song of creation in my head revolving

2

Who can stop this sacred song
that chains heart to heart?
this song that defies the seer hard to hear?
This song that forbids discord
but thrives in lasting accord?

O let not this be as those
which lie scotched like rose
trampled by passing years
Before it reaches the STAR

3

I am tired, tired!
my trembly feet drag.
Those in blood-bond
pass me by in their dream
And I, chastened by their passing
Drag my tired feet along
in pursuit of my own dream.

Celestial Song

Your song is celestial song
and so in "different plane"
mine is terrestrial song
and so is vain
vain, but it seeks ceaselessly
like rushing water the sea.
Let yours come down in drips
in crystal drips of starry light
to illumine the approaching night.

2

My song vainly climbs
like smoke from humble hearths.
It rises from lowly depths
to reach up to your song
but it is muffled by racing clouds.
So let yours come down in drips
just in drips, drips of starry song
To strengthen my trembly feet.

The Glowering Rat

This garden city lumbering out of a bad dream
sees ghosts in cooling wind and untended roses
struggling each to consummate its being.
And these puddles, these festering wounds
in streets and in my emptiness
over which my feet and mind totter
are presences cast like a shadow over my
every step; for a glowering Rat holds at bay
the spirit seeking its wonted lodgment.

But the spirit comes again and again
like homing bird, this spirit
with its wounded wings knocking coded
rhythms on resounding door, echoing
in capering hollowness; and again and again
the glowering Rat holds it at bay with bared
fangs and restive claws whetted on yesteryears.
And so dispossessed, the spirit waits restless
as unrecorded days pass into grumbling days
through fingers like drops of water into a turbulent river.

Port Harcourt, May 1970

The Dead a Spirit Demands

The dead a spirit demands
from the quick
in walls set
with mortar spewing words
from half-open lips,
A spirit that
these walls would break
and close their spittle specked
lips that despoil the land.
Yes, the dead such a spirit demands!

Christmas 1971

The name is strange, not strange
but not thoughts of love and peace
which have now donned
Simpleton's robes.
And caricatured, maligned
taunted and rejected
they ride in state on deriding tongues
with crown of thorns
forced on their heads
by gods assaulted and
by hidden fears of love and peace.
But love and peace will surely sprout skywards like a sapling
straight and strong from land
dripping with water from Pilate's hands.

Welcome Home

Welcome home to the fatherland
Flowing with milk, honey and oil
Where it's said one no longer needs to toil!
(But don't see my calloused palms,
See flabby hands shake flabby hands
Of kindred potentates with ingratiating smiles.
It's dangerous to see and say such things
Here where falsehood is standard balm!)

Welcome to the land free of mosquitoes
Ants and flies and dangerous creeping things
Where we no longer fear poisonous stings!
(But don't hear rejoicing mosquitoes singing at night
Or feel their sharp bites leaving itching, swollen
Skins, flying away laden with
Your precious blood. Don't ponder!
It's dangerous here to hear and think such things
Even when they sound like thunder.)

Welcome home to your fatherland
Flowing with milk, honey and oil
Where no one smiles without guile,
Makes counter choice aloud without fear of his genuine voice
Reaching ever-listening ears to trace and silence!

This, alas, it's not the land you left behind!
Things bedeviled, demonic, you'll now find
Displayed for unquestioning public praise
By disembodied mindless sycophantic voices.
So carefully tread; it's a strange land to your feet
For where you're made to stand may be a grave!

Welcome home again, I say, to your fatherland
Flowing with milk, honey and oil

Where it's said one no longer needs to toil.
But take not a welcome smile for a soulful smile
A beckoning hand for a friendly hand;
A chameleon, they say, may change its colors a million times
But it still is a chameleon!

Waiting for Her Son

She's been waiting for her son,
These twenty years she's been waiting,
Sitting on sand, at the waterside,
Since the drowning of the fleeting rising sun!

He went to war, jubilant,
To fight the Biafran "rebels" he said
Who had pillaged his riverside village!

He swore he would be brave and vigilant;
But twenty years have gone, wearily gone,
And tides have ebbed and flowed,
Making her wrapper wet and dry
Where she sits waiting to welcome her son,

She's been waiting for twenty years
Since the drowning of the Rising Sun!
Today she's lying on her back
Half awash in the river
And wavelets moving up and down her feet.

A smile of joy lightens her face,
And a look of recognition fixed on sightless eyes
With arms resting on her bosom!

She has, at last, seen her "boy"

30 September 1993

PART IV

Revolt of the Gods

Argument 1

FIRST GOD: We have died again and again
and have risen again and again
only to die again and again
in the dying whims of erratic modes
of man when man began and we
began with him countless centuries ago.
Since then we have owned the world
lost it, regained it and lost it
to the reckless mind of man.
He throws us to the mud, picks us up
refurbishes us, puts us in masks
stifling us, debases us in other guises
defaces us; gives us all powers
and takes them away,
as the mood catches him;
and kills us as sacrifice to his groping mind.

SECOND GOD: We grope along with man's mind
and go whither it bids us go and do
what it bids us do, helpless like
these clouds that clothe us, driven
hither and thither by the wind.
And now he bids us die. And we must die!

Argument 2

OLD GOD: It's death not sudden or final
    as you know. But as always it's suspension
    in mists of suffocating doubts
    which swing us high up to the heavens
    and down to the very dust he tramples on.
    And for centuries we've lived in this fashion
    We've lived in the twilight of life and death.

YOUNG GOD: Must you allow yourselves to die thus
    and live thus? Must you man's plaything
    remain to be discarded and retrieved at will?
    Man is a child. He must be controlled
    and guided. Power is burning in our hands like the sun
    Or have you by your quiescence
    changed roles and he is now your master?

OLD GOD: You speak like the young of god
    or man. By the grace or curse of man
    you came into being only a thousand years ago
    Many there were like you who died
    before they came or lived only
    a while and died in ignorance
    or simply wasted away for lack of sacrifices.
    Those who man loves are ageless.
    Those who he hates die ageless.
    Before long you will see this like the black
    cloud over there. We are powerless with all our power.
    We are powerless with our lightning and thunder.

SECOND GOD: Man's love is our curse
    His hatred is our grace!

YOUNG GOD: I can strike him down at will
   I can set fear on him like fire
   I can make him do my will
   I can make him weep and still
   his restless brain and bemoan his inadequacy
   And tears will gut his face like streams
   the face of the earth.
   All this power is you and I. You and I
   own the world, the universe and we
   step from planet to planet like the
   steps on stones to cross a stream.
   Yet, yet all this power, you say is useless —
   Now look down there and see him
   to whom you raise pleading hands.

   (The old gods peer down and there on earth
   man kneeling on dust, face upturned
   with hands clasped
   on his chest in sorrow and anguish
   is praying for the life of his dying child, dying
   before a shrine.)

   See now, see now on whom you
   dissipate your powers in plaintive words
   endowing him with powers beyond him
   making him bigger than himself
   See him melting in anguish
   like palm oil in fire
   Hear him crying, moaning
   See his prayers spiraling up
   like a bubble from sea's bottom.
   This is man you worship in your dotage.

SECOND GOD: Impetuousness of youth is the wisdom of age.

FIRST GOD: Storm agitates sea into restless waves
    Youth impels man or god into rashness.

YOUNG GOD: We are gods of the heavens and the universe
    Man and his abode are but a grain of sand
    in a desert, a drop of water in the limitless seas
    We drive into fury with our breaths
    Our whisper strikes fear and joy into him
    Our whisper caresses his mind and brain
    into illusions of grandeur beside himself
    And yet this grandeur with which he clothes
    himself is but a feather a gentle wind
    blown away at our command.

SECOND GOD: The interminable cycle of life and death
    lends caution to boasts of boundless power
    This truth in a million cycles
    you'll find entrenched
    And even now as we hold this discourse
    Man is soiling our virtues, obliterating, burnishing
    according as his convulsed mind turns and twists
    like a blind worm on heated sand.
    Now tune your ears to earth and hear
    their discourse rising in fumes of wine.

(*The young god cocks his ears downward*)

FIRST MAN: Don't tell me anymore, it spoils my drink.
SECOND MAN: The matter with you is you don't want to think.
FIRST MAN: What do you want me to think about?
    You want me to go raving mad and shout
    in the streets with my snout like swine?
    Allow me to drink in peace. My God is my wine.

THIRD MAN: Hear! Hear! Very well spoken. Here's to you!

FOURTH MAN: Now listen all of you, listen!

ALL: Yes, yes.

FOURTH MAN: I am a prophet!

SECOND MAN: Like the prophets of old?

FOURTH MAN: A prophet, a prophet
Prophet of Doom! Seer of Doom!

THIRD MAN: Hear! Hear! Well spoken. Here's to you!

FOURTH MAN: (*with a serious mien*) Fill my glass

SECOND MAN: What is your prophecy, may I ask, Prophet?

FOURTH MAN: (*sipping his drink*) Those who have ears to hear let
them hear

THIRD MAN: Hear! Hear!

FOURTH MAN: The world is coming to an end and all men should
their affairs attend.

FIRST MAN: (*cynically*) How is the world going to end?

FOURTH MAN: The gods have so decreed
And I enjoin you all to heed
this solemn message of the gods.

FIRST MAN: (*laughing*) They are all duds, duds.
Figments of your imagination!
There are no blinking gods.

SECOND MAN: (*solemnly*) But there is a God, the living God
of Abraham and his Son, Jehovah
The God of heaven and earth!

THIRD MAN: Hear! Hear! Well spoken. Here's to you! (*Drinks*)

FIRST MAN: Man is lord of the universe
He strides from earth to moon
and from moon to Mars and planets diverse
If there be God or gods then he is God or gods
And the world will only end when he so desires

THIRD MAN: Hear! Hear! Well spoken. Here's to you! (*Drinks*)

FOURTH MAN: All you doubting Thomases
will be thrown to the unquenchable
fire of hell. Soon, before you know it.

FIRST MAN: Thomas had a scientific mind

    Grow up man, grow up and free

    yourself from the shackles of your own creations.

THIRD MAN: Hear! Hear! Well spoken. Here's to you! (*Drinks*)

OLD GOD: That's how we are caught in the interminable cycle.

YOUNG GOD: Nonsense.

SECOND GOD: Even as you speak, your voice

    has weakened a trifle

    you are in earthly voices fading. . . .

OLD GOD: There's naught in your vaunted powers

    there's no choice

    And thus we suffer pains of a million deaths.

PART V

The Dreamer, His Vision

The Dreamer

He was seeking good in our collective good
As he stood aside, not apart, watching
Helpless stream of mankind passing slowly by;
Cheerless mankind with dying hopes of flickering flames
And sightless eyes staring at senseless toes, asking why?
Toes gnarled, twisted by dusty brown years of marching, waiting!

They took weary step by weary step and now skeptical steps,
Short steps cut short by fading visions of promised plenty;
But nudged on by limping hope they trudged forward,
Forward they trudged in timeless stream of time in seriatim
Without dreams of coming obstacles of twist and turns untoward,

On they trudged even as dreams turned malignant nightmares
Of waterless taps, empty pots, fireless fireplaces,
Of powerless power, authority overpowered by inch-thick darkness,
Yielded power to insistent generators to proclaim aggressive
Arrogance of wealth, snoring frog-like, in fear fortified homes.

So darkness their insidious mate became — the marching masses;
Sleepless heat their nightly fare became — the marching masses;
Worthless naira their bane became — the marching masses;

Sweat-soaked pariah naira made pariah by crafty shovel-hand
Of masked greed and lurid bags and pockets in gaudy world display!
Now rejected, shunned, it roams pariah regions, valueless,
Lying in pools of crumpled hopes in highway potholes, floating away

Tossed up or down in macro-fiscal turbulence by former peers,
Left million hearts beating fast in hope or slowly in despair, hopeless.

As he stood, the dreamer weighed, surveyed, tramping stamping
Mass of feet carrying bodies sapped by SAP to the bones
Like long trekking starving cattle with only skin hanging on bones
Led by swagger-stick babanriga cowherds in shining crushing boots,
A voice, the anguished voice of humanity rang out a questioning

Where's our common soul placed in your hands?
Where's our common laughter kept in vaults, silos of our land?
Where's our essence you pledged to guard uphold and enhance?

But swagger-stick babanriga demagogues in terminal narcissism
These questions ignored in double-chinned silence
As bubbles of air rising in river grow bigger and bigger,
As the bursting point comes nearer and nearer
So bigger and bigger grew their heaving stomachs
And bigger and bigger grew their insatiate greed,
And stoked people's anger long cooped in distending balloons,
Of colored slogans, multicolored slogans, of unkept promises
Like coming rainstorm-dark clouds over darkening horizon
    spreading!

So hotter and hotter grew glowing embers of resolute anger
As danger drums began to send lightning messages,
Slowly, slowly faster and faster sounded the drums
Blowing to flaming embers of defiance, and awakening
And massive feet of indomitable resolve moved forward as one
Impregnable march with souls in bruised emotions!

Slowly, slowly faster, faster and faster they ran, the people ran,
As louder and louder sounded the drums, the danger drums
Silencing countering syncopated praise drums of sycophants
And unmasked swagger-stick babanriga demagogues in smiling
    masks!

Thus exposed they made an offering of gilded dialogues,
Patchwork dialogues, in dribbling fiesta to dazzle
The land with tinseled brilliance in ambiguities and paradoxes
To dazzle, stupefy it once more into stupor languor as before.

But this frenzied hypnotic fiesta of juggling dialogues
Was dance of death, of tyranny, sneaky tyranny
Foisted in stealth on gullible land, an emasculated land!

So the Dreamer, with popular steps, strode forth,
Quickly merged with the massive march — a flag, an ensign
Of corporate will and might and claimed the right of our land!

And now the dreamer, with machete,
Word-sharpened, is clearing the forest
Of its macro-stench and venality
To sow the seed that would send its roots,
Unshaken by wind or storm, to its expected greatness.

May 1993

Bent Double with Weight

Bent double with weight
Our backs ached — we moaned
Our heads split — we moaned
We moaned for time to lift the alien weight
From our shouting backs, flexing
Muscles taut with aspirations of our due rights!
We shouted as one in diversity
And reluctant hands signed a deed of rights!

That was one score and eleven years ago
When we walked with backs straight and heads high
And looked straight in the eyes of the world
With our proud euphoric eyes daring all and sundry!
But that springy step is long gone.

We still walk with heads high but with lips pressed
On teeth, not with lifting an alien weight long gone,
But one imposed within by kith and kin — with license,
Threatening to devour our corporate body!

Darkness

We are now in darkness
Darkness fraught with aught
But dangers out of our fears;
We are in illusions of darkness
Illusions of twisting grimacing
Dangers herding our galloping hopes
Like unguarded cattle running wild
Away from the slaughterhouse!

We are now in darkness
And we are peering to see through
Darkness, listening and perceiving
With our sensitized senses,
Sounds unheard and things unseen in the light
But be calm, be calm, listen and wait!

The Precipice

I do not know what to say
(Unlike our humble martyrs)
This yawning precipice
At this point in timeless time
Threatening to swallow faith
In fellow men and women,
This dark cloud threatening.
I do not know what to say
Only that would men believe in
Humanity and love
There would be no rains, no precipices.
Only sunshine!
There would be no peering into faces
To divine what is behind the mask!
A smile would then be a smile,
A laugh a laugh, welling from the depths of being
Like a spring from the depths of the earth.

August 1976

Moon Massaged Me to Sleep

The moon peeped in at the window
As I lay tossing in bed trying to know
The loving touch of a mother
Which calms her restless baby child.
The moon massaged me to sleep.
I slept dreaming of walking
On moon beams with steps
Tender, eager, joyous and light
Into space where greed and
Venality have become fossils
Of an age long gone dead!

Adieu!

Adieu! Humanity that has failed me
Adieu! All that which lit my path
In this tunnel of echoing sounds of conflicts,
All that which reached out and grasped me
By the arm to show me the way — Adieu!

But a small sharp sound, sharp as the point of a needle,
The tiny voice of the bird I hear piercing
The clatter of a restless dawn, the sharp sound
Stabs the heart and I see the eyes of children,
The truck pusher, the farmer shuffling to his cassava
Farm, the fisherman paddling centuries old
Canoe to his fishing ground, the blind beggar
With his alms bowl and staff, knocking at hearts,
Unyielding hearts of humanity!

I see all those haunted eyes in the tunnel,
Unseeing eyes. I see them tripping,
Shoving aside the impeding faithful. I see them all
seeking reassurance as I seek mine to strengthen
my waning faith, waning in this deluge of darkness.

Anthem of Silence

In the silence of midnight silence
I heard the anthem of silence —
It silenced frogs; and mosquitoes
Kept their distance in silence!
It silenced the night!
And I, like one caught unawares
By one's national anthem, stood suddenly still
Encircled by this anthem of silence at midnight.

October 1993

Complex Matter

I am not one person, I am many things, many persons
I am what you see and think you know;
I am what I see and think I know of me —
I am many things many persons, known and unknown or
nearly known.

I sing with the singing dawn
And wake with the singing birds —
As with singer of dirges
The smile of a new day
As that of a first birthday!

I am a gently pacing morning —
Clearing horizons with a broom
Of silk-cotton strands, delineating
The shapeless, the amorphous
Promising fulfillment of yesterday's hopes.
I am not what you think you know;
I am the sun by day and the moon by night
Light the trackless dark for groping feet.
Of me this I like best —
I am an iroko tree, hard and strong
Defying storms and dagger-sharp words —
Stand serene above storms!
I wish I could be this all the time. . . .

27 December 1976

Dispensing Morning Balm

The rumble and asthmatic
Whizzing of the young day
Wakes me from dreams —
Nightmares of the fading darkness.

But these birds with crystal
Drops of songs dispensed from
Their liquid throats erase these
Nightmares of the receding night.

Setting Sun

See the moving triumph of blazing colors
Which the dusty mist of harmattan
Cannot hide, adorn the Western sky!
See it descending slowly into a bank of scurrying clouds,
And trees, misty gray trees, in the far horizon
Like impatient hands, are moving upwards
With a thick dark curtain!
And the sun, descending,
Slips silently in obedience behind the
Stretched-out darkness, leaving
Behind only traces of color to entice
Hearts to dreams of lasting beauty.

17 February 1987

Beauty beyond Words

The sun is sinking slowly in chanting colors!
And into yielding river of red and orange
I move my despoiling paddle
Like defacing brush on beautiful painting in oil,
As waters part with yielding murmur
And canoe moves in silent obedience.
It moves silently into colored shadows
As parting water turns parting colors
In wavelets radiating from glow
Of sun when it meets a waiting river!

15 September 1995

Taps Are Dry

Hopes long drawn thin, long gone
For taps and faucets to hiss with water,
Of the times there were, when no thoughts were spared
To keep running water running from taps
In houses and squares to rid
Us of lingering thirst and intimidating dirt
In hearts for human dignity.

Self Preservation

(To Ken Saro-Wiwa — Hanged Humans Rights Campaigner)

Tomorrow is year to promised year,
Year of freedom from strife and venality;
But offensive clamor is threatening to silence
Yet unsounded drums of dormant hopes, questions; ...
And challenges yet to rise from compost heap of dead promises,
Which have dehumanized proud vibrant land
Into grotesque parody of its once exalted self!

And now like a woman accused
Of killing children, her own, with witch-craft,
The land stands petulant, unrepentant, alone,
In circle of accusing eyes, claiming she's been abused
wrongly for that "little act" of self preservation!

The Little Bird

Sing, little bird, as always
In early mornings, dispensing
Joy in the fragrance
Of frangipani flowers wafted
By the morning wind
To freshen hearts filled
With ill-smelling hate!

Sing of your liberty and love
O you inhabitants of the wind!
You cannot but sing of love and freedom.

So I can also sing that which
Filters into my heart, like sunrays,
Through unnoticed chinks in a wall!
But mine's a forbidden song.
And so I sing only in whispers
Some feeble words unheard
By a land deadened by fears and din of conflicts.

Morbidity

Why do they smile
With the rising sun after the rains?
Why do the birds sing
In my window in the gently moving
Leaves of the trees this morning?
Why do they smile?
Why do they smile?
I do not see the sun
To feel the quickening warmth,
I do not hear the raining rain
Nor the after-rain songs of birds.
I am engulfed by the miasma
Of human whims, the Creek Road swamps
Which defy the cleansing rains!

Smiling Morning

This is smiling morning
With the kindly rays of the sun
Skimming the tops of trees
And the stream, fanned by the gentle wind
Turns specks of shimmering silver foils!
And the birds, in accord, sing their morning songs of adoration
Of love, free from debilitating hate,
Preen their feathers to let in the morning sun.

Yet I feel but cold in this joyous morning,
I am being estranged by complex humanity,
Humanity gorged with dreams of adulation
Render up my faith on a platter fashioned
With perfidy to their god for honor!
But what is honor starved of life-giving truth?
It is corn starved of its sap!

River Nun — 2

Flowing like the thoughts
Of a cloistered nun
Or that in a seminary,
The River NUN
Runs deep and shallow,
But tempted out of its course
It splits in its languid flow
Isolating land and thoughts
Into islands of ripening corn

Or flowering sugar-cane
And impeding elephant grass!
Then it finds again its way, its course,
Lower down at last, and flows deep
Into the deep unfathomable
Depths of light, in (Kiabara) shimmering brightness,
Where no more mysteries exist,
Like the cloistered nun who has made
Her last saintly genuflection,
Pressing her crucifix to her bosom
In total submission to what only the saints see!

We Live to Kill and Kill to Live

Hiroshima, Nagasaki — bombs
Holocaust, Germany
Genocide, Bosnia Herzegovina, nuclear bombs!
Rwanda, Burundi, Genocide, fragmentation bombs.
Advancing weapons of mass destruction.
Oppressions, suppressions, aggression, bombs!

We live to kill
And kill to live!
Oppress, suppress to live,
And live to oppress, suppress
With our many inventions
Without any pretensions

We live to kill,
And kill to live

So, impelled by hate and fear and greed
We test:

In our heads,
Above sea,
Above ground,
Under sea,
Under ground,
Weapons for self-extinction
With no single distinction
Of race, color, creed, or religion!

17 September 1995

The Land at Christmas '93

Strong harmattan winds are blowing
But June twelfth cannot be blown away!
Though dust-filled eyes and battered minds
Wander in wilderness of desires away from Xmas,
June twelfth cannot be desired away!

The land has claimed manhood after ordeals
Of coups, greedy coups of fiefdom seekers
Rampaging looters; grabbing addiction for power!

An adult can't forget his manhood
However strong the cartel of harmattan winds,
June twelfth cannot be blown away!

It was the day the land woke triumphant
In final manhood rituals in mending
Its bruised, savaged, disparate members!

No! June twelfth cannot be blown away

However strong with self-consuming power-lust, the harmattan
    winds!
Hate and greed have never consumed the essence of Christmas.

Ovation Seeker

With drums beating and cymbals crashing
He went strutting, smiling from ear to ear,
He who seeks ovation, plaudits, like seeker of gold!
He went strutting and smiling with his absent ovation
Like the naked king with his absent robes
But with his ears filled with shouts of adulation
He led the absent crowd to the fallen,
Who fell by his injudicious hand!

He led the crowd of ghosts, strutting in front,
And with his fingers shaking with pride
He showed them where he thought the fallen lay!
But the fallen was not there!
The fallen was not fallen. For the people's voice
Had wakened him from illusion of a fall!
And so with ashes of a smile on his lips,
The seeker of ovation ambled away, still seeking!...

Mass Transit Buses

The governor's exhortations
Were their launching pad!
Away they careered!
The masses cheered!
Shed were tears of joy
From eyes firmly closed.
And when their eyes were opened
The buses from the streets had vanished!

They were a drop of cold
water on thirsty tongues of the masses
For whom the launching
Became only a wishful dream.

Contractors

Men and women
Wearing grim, ingratiating faces,
Moving with money-steps; and receptionists
With pothole-faces of money importance
Blocking or allowing them pass
The money checkpoints.

And each with steps fast or slow
Controlled by expectations or past experiences.
They shake money-familiar hands
With loud laughter and sudden lowering
Of voices to conspiratory whispers with

Eyes elsewhere, but not at one another,
Scanning flamboyant money-eyed throng
For business foes who must be stopped dead,
By "settled" officialdom!
And with assured ebullient steps
They walk past panting fellow money seekers
Into an office with naira smiles
Standing behind a familiar desk!

Civil Servants

They went counting manual days.
Now we are counting electronic days!
But just counting days,
The same crawling days,
As we crawl up stairs
Away or down, in or out,
From piling files.
With urging minutes
"IMMEDIATE ACTION," in red!

It's no secret in our secret cult —
The higher the pile of files left untouched
In the IN tray the quicker
You are in your UP-TAKE!
Or intelligence, in
Civil service terminology.

So we count days and days
Restless days and mounting files
For credit, while spending on credit

To await the crawling "P" day
With its leaden feet!

Smokers' Wish

With heads buried in swirling
smoke of cigarette, they
raise their smoked thoughts
in gratitude to tobacco leaves,
the farmers and planters,
and wish them (panting heavily for breath)
a richer harvest next harvest time!

Man Dies, Never Dies

Some say man never dies
Others say he certainly does
So man dies, never dies
As Christ died, never died.

Some say the sun shines unseen at night
And the moon unseen at noon
So the sun and moon set, never set
Behind trees, hills and seas
Or beyond hazy horizons at dusk.

So laboring days and tireless months
Pass like a moving surveyor's chain

Marked in millimeters, centimeters and meters.

Years crawl, limp or joyously caper past
In relentless single file, through nightmares,
Mirages in eternal cycles of symbols, similes
And predictions of when fiery sun would stand still
And nerve-mending moon never would rise again!

So we live or die as sooth-sayers
Cowry throwers or grim-faced star gazers
(with our fear-weary selves)
Feebly looking forever for illusive life's essence.

PART VI

Prayers and Tributes

Give Us Good Leaders

O God, give us leaders!
But not those who would
Sit round their soup
In golden pots and
With an arrogant sweep
Of their hands
Spill ours in our
Earthen pots!

Or
Those in their lofty heights
Would spit on our lowly heads!

O God, give us leaders
Men and women
Who would feed us
With seven loaves of bread!

May 1993

Talking Nonsense

I'm talking non-sense?
You are thinking, not thinking?

You stare at nothing.
What's the sense in talking sense,
Staring at nothing?
You say I'm talking non-sense
Even before I open my mouth!
Those who talk non-sense also
Have shoulders carrying their heads.
What's the sense in talking sense
When there's no sense around?
Sense has long left us without sense
So we talk and do non-sense things
And you, staring at spiraling smoke of incense,
Dream of the return of prodigal sense!

Port Harcourt, 1990

Rural Dweller

It's cock-crow!
She draws her aching limbs
On her creaking bamboo bed;
And once again to the farm she must go,
As she has done at every cock-crow
Since these months of sowing before the rains.
Her face lined with furrows of labor

And her hands calloused and fingers
Twisted like scraggy roots of a hillside tree,
For her oil lamp she gropes
In the morning darkness
As the sound of passing lorries
Fails to drown the song of early birds
From far and near, filling the morning air
With gladdening sounds,
But the sounds pass her by unheard
For her mind is stuck on her hoe!

At last she stands outside her hut
Of wattle and mud, gazing at the morning sky.

The trees slowly take form, drawn
By the rising sun and woken to life by the wind,
They sway back and forth in time
With rhythm unheard, unseen in the morning sky.
And weakened by age, her feet tremble, but with steps
Tradition-urged, she goes her wonted way to the farm
With a hoe, untouched by time, in a basket, on her head.
Thus she walks with no lodgment in her thoughts
Of promised changes for the better at dawn
As she turns off the asphalt road into a foot path,
Seen only by her uncluttered mind and
tradition-taught vision!

20 June 1978

Lone Mourner

Strapped firmly on to her back,
her child innocently asleep,
she walked sobbing silently
following a crude, "cut and nail" coffin
of abura wood carried by a carrier
with rivulets of sweat running down
his forehead and bare chest.

Urged by the weight of his burden
the carrier quickened his steps;
she also quickened her steps.
The child snapped open its eyes
and shut them slowly, lulled
by the rhythm of mother's hastening feet.

She wiped her face of dust and tears
as she looked down at the coffin being lowered
and asked with tear-filled eyes
to see her husband for the last time.
Grumbling grave-digger quickly opened and shut the coffin.

The lone mourner with moving lips
Turned and walked away, adjusting weight
Of still sleeping child on her back,
She walked away with grim steps never looking back!

Apartheid

The god from the south
may threaten brimstone,
fire, hell, the perverted image of man impose!
Nothing halts the rising sun at dawn
Not even Apartheid, the god of the south!

15 June 1987

Spark in the Sky

(On the death of my gifted granddaughter)

There she was,
like the sun in its glory
at dawn with the promise
of perfect noon and marvel
of approaching evening.

Her horizontal steps
were the living rays
outlining shapes of the universe
beyond imperfect human concepts —
concepts which are mere
counterfeits of perfect ideas
above the confines of time and space

Somewhere there she fixed
her gaze, severe and intense!

She moved fast above wondering heads
With garlands of joy and wonder,
Manifesting divine gifts.

But struck down in her youthful stride
by imperfect devices of man seeking the speed of mind
she became only a promise unfulfilled, hers and mine
Just a mere spark in the sky!

18 October 1985

A Prayer

(In Tribute to Sister Mary)

O Lord, I do not know,
I do not know what to say
about one I do not know
Yet I know by her flowering tree of love
planted fifty years ago.

I do not know,
I do not know what to say
But this:
     The light of the tree of love
     illumines hearts and minds
     of even those who watch from afar
     from distances of seeming schisms
     of an indivisible seamless Robe!

Really, I do not know,
I do not know what to say
but again this, Lord:
    May Thy Spirit, which was in Sister Mary
    Be also in those who now selflessly tend
    this undying tree of flowering love.

And this, Lord:
    Let even those who watch from afar
    sniff this fragrance of immortal flowers.

O Lord, forgive me
I do not have more to say for
the brightness of infinite love
overwhelms my groping heart!

From Ken to Mike

Hear this my friend
from a face last seen,
a voice last heard in '82:
Like suya meat half-done, charred or rotten
pierced together for the palate's pleasure,
To you I offer skewered essence of years
With accompanying mouth odors
Of rulers' loud protestations of innocence
As delectable fare and seasonal remembrances!

10 February 1997

Rise and Shine

Rise and Shine, O shine
like resplendent morning, sun;
Open our hearts, our yearning hearts
and receive the healing blessings
coming from above like raindrops
to us His image and likeness
with his boundless lovingkindness.

Let's rise and shine,
and bless our father-mother God
for daily manna of angel thoughts
sent down continually in endless flow
of gentle showers or love from love
to assuage our prodding hunger
for Truth, that we may hunger no longer.

Let's shine, therefore shine
with the Christ illumining our hearts
And through us to others in selfless sharing
till error's dark and limiting shadows disappear
as all mankind see the light of Truth —
our father-mother God — the truth of Truth!

Requiem

All who love our beloved land
bow your heads in leaden sorrow;
for Mohammed has fallen by assassin's hand
an assassin whose evil purpose we know
but also this we know: he has wrought with his wicked hand
a deed that has torn our hearts asunder with grief
as we in desolation deeply mourn Muritala and our land.

O let us mourn our beloved Mohammed
who beckoned us unto the path he had set
with sturdy feet and unflinching heart!

Let us mourn him who like a star in the sky
in dark and somber clouds in a dark night
illumined this land's dark and threatening sky.
O let us weep, but let not our tears
Bedim that torch, that beacon, that marks our course.

Let it shine forth from our hearts
And minds to the illumined horizon and beyond —
For this will be our greatest tribute to Ramat
Though laid to rest, he still lives on
In the seed in our hearts he has sown with his blood.

1976

Man Polygamous

Man by nature is polygamous, they say,
Try not to be, you battle with futility
And become increasingly glamorous
As you recognize its vast utility
In appeasing impatient masculinity.

Still you vow to be monogamous
While leading strenuous life polygamous —
Serving neither as true devotee.

So you are not this or that in reality;
But are counted among the infamous
By those claiming to be virtuous,
For being an initiate of the cult of two-stoolers
And the bubbling throng of befoolers!

Mammy-Water & Me

The embers are smoldering — once again —
They've refused to die into *in memoriam* ashes —
And have burst into flames I cannot temper.
They draw into their whirling vortex, helpless —

Mammy-water & me.

There we stand, hand in hand,
Like Shadrach and company, the faithfuls,
Calmly waiting for the redeeming flames

To do the cleansing and free us of earthly dross!
Then we shall step out with solemn steps
To silence offended eyebrows and daggered tongues
and walk on calm waters — still, serene — Free!

Mammy-water & me.

Wedding Bells

(To Ezekiel and Peace)

May the bell keep ringing
Peace and happiness keep bringing
Even when harsh sun at noon
Tends to silence the bell sounds
May the bell keep ringing!
To usher in the glory of a setting sun.

18 December 1982

To the Lady of the House

(A Wedding Gift)

Though this be late, it no less ensures
A smiling wedlock state.
If for no reason you can espy
(None they usually have)

He goes boiling, foaming by,
Just boil that which he most desires
And serve up smiling with this set
And be sure, a breed he'll sire
Of your heart's uppermost desire!

For Ada Udechukwu

Happy birthday, Ada, our Ada
I wish you many happy returns of good cuisine
Igbo cuisine, Ofe Onugbu, Nni aka.
I knew my friend before you
In very trying times in other places,
He likes it hot, Ada,
Right from the pot, Ada,
So don't you dare him
With something cold.
He'll explode to the sky.
You can't then ask why
For you know he likes it hot,
Best of all
Let him take it direct from the pot
Then he'll be content
By repeatedly saying
"what the madman said
what the madman said."

Nsukka, 10 July 1990

A Boy's Dream

I cling to soft clouds swaying
In the wind as a swing
Clouds in soft colors reflecting
The slowly rising sun-moon succeeding—
I cling to soft clouds following the wind.

I cling to silk-cotton hopes, hoping
For moon-like smiles coming from glittering hearts
Glittering with faith and humanism, beckoning
With hands stretched out of the rising sun!

I stand at the beginning, delineating
Shapes and forms and thoughts and minds
With stimulating hopes and eyes not seeing
The difference in shades, tones and colors of sound—
All in one perfect harmonious blending!

And I dare not open my eyes in my waking
So I cling to soft clouds swaying
In the wind as in a swing
With warmth of the sun playing on my face.

22 July 1978

Queen

There she is, the queen
Sitting on the throne of a heart;
Though young and fresh
She reigns supreme; and
Not desirous of conflicts
Sweeps regally aside
All encumbrances, remembrances
Of the fast receding past.

And so there she sits,
Immovable, like a goddess
Before whom a supplicant
Kneels with his forehead resting on her feet.

Owerri, March 1995

Letter to My Grandson

(Yet to Be Born)

My dear Grandson,
I hear you are coming son, soon,
Soon after the wedding fiesta and laughter
In answer to our calls the morning after,
Calls we made in prayer unvoiced just before noon.

The one who's sending you hastening
Will ensure a joyous homecoming

As there will be many a heart a-welcoming
On that tenth day of November, '93!

So let your yells be manly, loud and clear,
Echoing in distances unlimited so we may also hear
For that, we'll all be listening, a signal
To start celebrating your arrival in style!
P.S. Tell your sister to bide her time awhile;
Patience, a valuable virtue is, her turn will come after a year

Your Grand-Pa

August 1992

Babydom Wisdom

In India, 800 million Indians —
Men and women, walk in Indian file,
Men in front with hands clasped behind,
And women follow, meek and docile.

In Africa, 300 million Africans —
Men and women, walk in single file,
Men in front with chests thrust out,
And women follow, meek and docile.

In America and elsewhere
Men shout "Ladies First" in surface jubilation
Saying it's a hallmark of civilization;
But they laugh with their bellies in full appreciation
When professional emcee announces "Mr. and Mrs. Winterbottom!"

Woman is nudged into her niche in babydom wisdom!
But to her the reversal unclear, she joins the clapping throng
With ready-made smile playing on her sophisticated lips!

To women's "Libbers," past and present, my apologies sincere!
For we merely are echoing wisdom of babies which they too once
     were
so let not their ambition wane or their spirit be troubled;
still to them remains their consummate art of persuasion
which they could harness, at will, into baby-song play
to lull their babies out of their babydom wisdom!

But till then,
it's Da da da
Before
Mamama!

January 1993

Waiting for a Coming

As silent as the silent snow
On the silent ground, a lone leaf winter-dried
Scampered, pushed by the playful winter-wind
Which blew aside the feeble rays of the morning sun.

And she snow fell unhindered on ground and roofs
Of houses hushed by frozen winter-silence
And stolid elms bear their cyclic witness
With leafless branches like skeletal fingers
Spread in the face of winter-befuddled sun

As they await with mute joy, the coming of summer!

So deprived squirrels also wait in their winter holes
Feeding on gathered fruits and nuts and instinct
For the same coming fore-ordained in animal lore.

Man too waits feeding on hope, faith and prophecy
For the coming of his Savior

Milton, USA, 5 February 1993

Snow over Home of the Newly Wed

Crystals in clusters of white confetti
Spiral down on home of the newly wedded
And fusing with others already there
Present a spectacle of heavenly white
Never imaged in human mind!

Let this heavenly snow be cleansing agent
And its cold cool the minds of the violent
Who've paved streets with fear
Where the gentle and innocent fear to tread!
O let its freshness and purity
Embrace minds in all climes
And be guarantee for peace, happiness
For all newly wed and new-born child in all lands!

Milton, USA, 1993

Before I Say Goodbye (India)

Before I say goodbye let me make a confession;
Creeping slowly up my emotions
Is a thought that makes me shudder
As with the cold of Bhopal
Or with the warmth of Vagarth.
I shudder not because of the enormity of the thought
Nor because it is unthinkable
Or because it is unattainable
But I shudder with hope
Because of the one humanity deep down in our hearts
Which has brought us together and which
Transcends all man-made walls of slogans and ideologies!
Still I shudder because as always,
Emotions are not the best of guardians
Of human reality. They tend rather to make
One walk in the air; see mountains
As powdery sand one shovels out of the way;
Rocky valleys as paved highways;
And seas separating continents as non-existent;
Yet I don't want to think of self-evident reality;
For human reality often tends to masquerade inner reality
So let's walk hand in hand in our joyful emotions
And in the eternal vista of our common humanity —

Goodbye . . . !

Bhopal, India, 16 January 1989

Moon over Heidelberg

Hanging from the vast night sky
Like a Chinese lamp glowing
Over a festive street, the moon's
Luminous rays like gentle hands
Smooth the pockmarked years on
The rough-hewn stones of Heidelberg castle.

The echoes of sword-drawn challenges
From stout hearts within and without
Which bounced from rugged walls
To parapets guarded with impatient
Bow and arrow and anxious whispers
Are now heard no more but only in history.

They are now silent
As the calloused hands are still
Which hewed the stones for this monument
Of romanticism now mummified only in the silence
Of floodlights and the moon over Heidelberg.

1963, 1992

Salt of the Earth

They wore the mark of recognition —
The weight-folds and care-lines
On foreheads, fingers hard
And rough like the twisted roots
Seeking water in the hard and dry rocks!

I saw them in single file, walking
With flowing sarees once colorful and bright
But now brown with dust and grime

They walked up the slope, carrying
On their heads heavy rocks chipped
Out of surrounding hills.

Here houses are built not on sand
But on patient rocks which had been
From the beginning (here too man is pointing
the way to his forgotten beginning).
And these women of the earth, the whole
Earth, whose graceful steps still reveal
Their youthful elegance and zest for life,
Howbeit ever so wearily, can afford
The warmest of guileless smiles in return
For the slightest wave of the hand in mute greeting
And their nose-rings sparkle in the sun

Mount Abu, India, 2 February 1989

Eagle in the Sun

Granite etched Bird in the sun,
A message from eternal past
With an echoing song of the ages
That built these walls of stone
Bids man to gaze in awe and be still

Be still and listen to the compelling song
With living rhythms, stringing centuries like beads
Round a maiden's comely neck
Admired and admiring as it
Erases a lingering myth from human mind.

So turn not this creative song of the Bird
Into a dirge, O, man, be still and listen!
It may erase another yet. Be still and listen!

Ancient Walls of Zimbabwe, 10 September 1985

The Aruzzo Farm House

High on the hills of Sicily
Stands the Aruzzo farm house
Shrouded in the silence of centuries
Pressing hard to be of the moment.

But its gray rugged exterior
Belies stately halls and shining floors within
With paintings by artists now unknown, gone, dead

And with photographs of sires, proud, serene,
Hanging on walls from which
The centuries have been washed away.

Though the walls are silenced by
The hasty hands of the iconoclasts
They whisper loudly the dreams of yesteryears.

Sicily, 1992

We Shared

(Dedicated to My Friend Ezenwa-Ohaeto)

What can i say
What can i say
Of a master drummer
Whose drum went suddenly silent?
With drumsticks falling away
From limp fingers no longer able to stay the
inevitable?

Only this:

We shared a life of drums and drummers
We shared a class of drummers at IMOSU
We shared the prize of champion drummers

We more can i say
Of one who pelted out messages
Embedded in indigenous drum-beat cadences

To jolt unaccustomed ears to listen in wonder
What more, what more, can i say

Than this:

We shared a stage
We shared a standing ovation
We shared the spotlight,

As we stood clinging to one another
In an embrace of joy never thinking of parting
But he departed without waving,
Not even with his nimble drumsticks,
Not even a whispered goodbye!

Happy Birthday

To Nigeria, on the Fiftieth Anniversary of Her Independence, 1 October 2010

Happy birthday, my land, my nation:
You have endured five decades
of tribulation and turbulence
subdued by "militant materialism"
your "Canoe of Hope" had swayed
from side to side, turned in all
directions but the true; for the pilots
had become ardent acolytes of the new
god of self-esteem and daring self service!

Yet our "Canoe of Hope" remained afloat!
But the people disoriented moved

round and round myriad options
for a pilot to redirect our "Canoe of Hope"
away from the path of self-destruction.

Men and women, our search
is ended; for God is, God is able and
has chosen one who would perform
the miracles of change for a joyful hate-less nation.

So shout "Happy Birthday" with your love
for the reign of the chosen is at hand:
I see him striding down the horizon
with garland of stars —
Integrity, Sanity, Honesty, Transparency,
Due Process — shining around his neck
stepping with sure and steady feet
to assert his reign by the people's voice
and Due Process!

So let's let go the past and its adherents
and welcome the miracle of change
with joy; and as we celebrate, God is,
and God blesses only those who work for the
general good of the governed.

The death of an era is the birth of another
and in the new, we can claim
without blemish our deserved
seat among the great nations
of the world!

Happy Birthday, Nigeria!

Canton, Massachusetts, 23 September 2010

abura. A typically orange-red wood from tropical West Africa, used in cabinetmaking and flooring.

Adhiambo. Adhiambo Carmichael Okara, an African American and Chicagoan of Jamaican heritage, was the third and last wife of the author, and died in 1983 at Port Harcourt, Nigeria.

Aladuras. Members of a Nigerian Christian sect practicing ritual bathing.

Apartheid. Afrikaans (South African Dutch) term for the racist policy of segregation practiced in South Africa until the emergence of majority rule in 1994, when Nelson Mandela became the nation's first black president.

Babalawo. Priest-diviner in traditional Yoruba religion and its transatlantic derivatives, such as Santería, Palo Mayombe, and Haitian Vodún.

babanriga. A type of expensive flowing robe of Arabian origin worn by the rich and powerful in Nigeria and elsewhere in West Africa.

Back. Ijaw language construct used to represent the past; its counterpart, *Front*, represents the future).

Bhopal (India). Large rural town in central India where 1982 Union Carbide chemical accident killed fifty-two hundred and injured many more.

Biafra. Republic of Biafra (1967–70), secessionist state comprising the Eastern Region of Nigeria's First Republic.

Biafran "rebels." Pejorative name for soldiers and supporters of Biafra during the Biafran War for Independence (1967–12 January 1970) employed by Nigerian federal media and propaganda.

Bofors. A World War II Swedish-manufactured antiaircraft weapon employed by Biafran navy.

Chest. The quality of courage central to Ijaw philosophy, religion, and worldview.

Creek Road. A street in Port Harcourt close to swamps that emit gaseous odor at low tide.

Dreamer. Alhaji Moshood Abiola, businessman and putative winner of the annulled Nigerian presidential elections of 12 June 1999, to whom the collection *The Dreamer, His Vision* (2004), is dedicated.

Enugu. Capital of Eastern Nigeria, where most of Okara's early poems were written and where he worked as bookbinder, information officer, and director of Information Services from 1956 to 1967.

Ezenwa-Ohaeto. Poet, short story writer, biographer, widely acclaimed as Nigeria's most prolific critic, Exenwa-Ohaeto was professor of English at Nnamdi Azikiwe University, Awka until his untimely death in Cambridge, UK, in 2007. In 2004 he shared the Liquefied Natural Gas (LNG) Prize for Nigerian Literature with Okara.

Front. *See* Back.

Harmattan. Cold, dry wind blowing from the Sahara Desert across West Africa in December and January.

Heidelberg Castle. Famed ruins and landmark of Heidelberg, Germany. The poem was written during the poet's visit to his daughter, then residing in Germany.

Icarus. In Greek mythology the son of the master craftsman Daedalus, who constructed wings of wax and feathers for himself and his son in order to escape captivity on the island of Crete. Icarus flew too close to the sun and drowned in the sea.

IMOSU. An acronym (also IMSU) for Imo State University.

iroko. The silk-cotton tree, a hardwood known as "King of Woods," common to the African rainforest and producing a species of brown wood favored in cabinetmaking as well as for outdoor use. The tree has strong religious significance, particularly among the Yoruba people.

Kiabara (Ijaw). Name of humanities journal published by the Faculty of Arts, University of Port Harcourt.

Kwashiorkor. A nutritional disorder resulting from insufficient protein intake. The disease is common to developing nations as a result of famine resulting from war, natural disaster, extreme poverty. Primarily affecting children, its most visible symptoms include recurrent diarrhea, extreme weight loss, fatigue, irritability, listlessness, and distended bellies. Originally, a Ghanaian word of Kwa or Ga language, referring to the loss of protein suffered by a first child deprived of mother's milk when a second is born soon after.

LMG. Light machine gun. Czechoslovakian-made weapon, designed in 1920s, used in Biafran War.

MIG. Acronym for Mikoyan-Gurevich (names of designers), a Soviet-manufactured twin-engine jet fighter aircraft employed during the Biafran War.

naira. The currency of Nigeria.

Ofe Onugbu. Bitterleaf soup; traditional Nigerian dish containing bitterleaf vegetable (*Vernonia amygdalina*), beef, fish, ground crawfish, cocoyam, and the traditional spice known as Ogiri Igbo. It is native to the Eastern Nigerian Igbo people and part of the diet also of the Hausa and Yoruba.

Ramat, Muhammed (General Murtala Rafai Mohammed) (1938–76). Head of the Federal Military Government of Nigeria from July 1975 until his assassination in February of the following year at age thirty-seven. Recognized as a national hero, he enjoyed wide popular support during his brief time in office. His portrait appears on the twenty-naira note, and the Lagos airport was renamed Murtala Muhammed National Airport in his honor.

River Nun. Located in southern Nigeria, one of two rivers created where the Niger breaks in two, creating both the Nun and Forcados Rivers. The Nun flows one hundred miles southeast to the Gulf of Guinea. Throughout the nineteenth century it was a major Ijaw trade route. Discovery of oil in the Niger Delta has since made it the site of protest against continued environmental abuses.

SAP. Acronym for Structural Adjustment Program, an austerity measurement imposed by the World Bank and International Monetary Fund (IMF) requiring devaluation of national currency, increased taxation, privatization of economic concerns, increased export, and limited government spending.

Saro-Wiwa, Kenule "Ken" Beeson (1941–95). Nigerian author, television producer, and human rights/environmental activist, founder of the Movement for the Survival of the Ogoni People; executed in 1995 by the Abacha government for his activism against Western oil conglomerates operating in the Niger Delta and the Nigerian federal government's complicity in environmental and human rights abuses.

Sister Mary. Roman Catholic nun who worked in Calabar, Nigeria.

suya meat. A national dish of Nigeria, made from a variety of grilled meats and served as an appetizer or dish with vegetables and condiments. Suya is highly spiced and often served on a skewer.

Udechukwu, Ada. Wife of Obiora Udechukwu, then a lecturer at the University of Nigeria, Nsukka. This tribute was written in the Udechukwu home at a dinner on the occasion of her birthday, which fell on the date of publication of *What the Madman Said*, Obiora's first book of poems.

CHRONOLOGY

"All the while . . . I was reading and writing."

1945–50   Printer and bookbinder, Government Press, Lagos.

Continues watercolor painting and nurses ambition to enter a career in fine art.

Experiences vision of recently deceased Nigerian nationalist Herbert Macaulay, who removes brush from his hand and leaves three books marked "Down, Down, Down." Begins intense study of poetry.

Inspired by Wordsworth's "Lines Written in Early Spring," begins writing poetry by translating traditional Ijaw lyrics into English.

Writes scripts for government radio.

1950   Transfers to Enugu as member of founding staff of new Government Press.

Composes "The Call of the River Nun," an *ubi sunt* poem treating life and culture of his native riverine Niger Delta community.

1952	Receives British Council Short Story Competition award (Nigeria–Eastern Region).
1953	"The Call of the River Nun" receives Nigerian Festival of the Arts Silver Cup for Best All-Around Entry in Poetry, Lagos.
1955–67	Information Services Officer, Eastern Nigerian Government, Enugu.
	Undertakes study at British Information Services Centre, London.
1957	"The Call of the River Nun" published in *Black Orpheus*; becomes one of the poet's most widely anthologized poems.
1958	January: "Ogboinba: The Ijaw Creation Myth," published in *Black Orpheus*.
1959	August: Enrolls in U.S. Foreign Journalist Program, Comparative Journalism and Public Relations, Medill School of Journalism, Northwestern University, Evanston, Illinois.
	Composes "The Snowflakes Sail Gently Down," a meditative poem in which snowbound African expatriate dreams an end to colonial exploitation of Africa.
1960	January: Foreign Journalist Certificate in Comparative Journalism.
	"The Crooks" (short story) published in *Black Orpheus*.
1962	Poems featured in *Reflections: Nigerian Prose and Verse*, ed. Frances Ademola (Lagos: African Universities Press).
1963	Attends UNESCO seminar on the Dissemination of Information in the Rural Areas of Third World Countries.
1964	January 4: "Tubi" (short story) published in *Flamingo*.
	The Voice (novel) published (London: André Deutsch / Heinemann Educational Books).
	"African Speech . . . English Words" (essay) published in *Transition III*.

Short story featured in *Modern African Stories*, ed. E. A. Komey and E. Mphahlele (London: Faber and Faber).

Attends Information Officer's Course, British Government Central Office of Information, London.

Featured in *Black Orpheus: An Anthology of New African and Afro-American Stories*, ed. Ulli Beier (New York: McGraw-Hill).

1964–67   Head of Information Services of Eastern Nigeria, Enugu.

1965   Attends UNESCO seminar on the Dissemination of Information in the Rural Areas of Third World Countries.

May: "Poetry and Oral English" (essay) published in *Journal of the Nigerian English Studies Association*.

Featured in *Pan African Short Stories: An Anthology for Schools*, ed. N. Denny (London: Nelson Thomas Learning).

1965–66   Visiting lecturer in the Use of English, General Studies, University of Nigeria, Nsukka, Enugu Campus.

1967   December: "Leave Us Alone" (poem) protesting atrocities against Eastern Nigerians by fellow Nigerians and calling for independent nation-state of Biafra, published, Government Printer, Aba, Abia State, Enugu.

Featured in *West African Verse: An Anthology*, ed. Donatus Ibe Nwoga (London: Longmans) and *Poems from Nigeria*, ed. Peter D. Thomas (New York: Vantage Press).

1967–69   Director of Information Services and Senior Executive Official of the Biafran Directorate for Propaganda.

1968   Travels widely in Europe and North America, with novelist Chinua Achebe and short story author Cyprian Ekwensi, as ambassador of goodwill for Biafra.

1969–70   Director, Cultural Division of the Propaganda Directorate of Biafra, coordinating wartime creative activity of writers, artists, and performers, at Ogwa.

1970   *The Voice* reprinted, with critical introduction by Arthur Ravenscroft (London: Heinemann).

1970–71   Personal assistant to governor of Rivers State.

1971–73   First general manager, Rivers State Newspaper Corp.

1972   Featured in *Africa Is Thunder and Wonder: Contemporary Voices from African Literature*, ed. B. Nolen (New York: Scribner).

1973   "African Speech . . . English Words" reprinted in *African Writers on African Writing*, ed. G. D. Killam (Evanston IL: Northwestern University Press).

1975   Featured in *Poems of Black Africa*, ed. Wole Soyinka (London: Heinemann).

1975–76   Commissioner, Information and Broadcasting, Rivers State Government.

1977   Featured in *Aftermath: An Anthology of Poems in English from Africa, Asia, and the Caribbean*, ed. R. Weaver (Greenfield Center NY: Greenfield Review Press).

1977–83   Writer-in-residence, Rivers State Council for Arts and Culture.

1978   *The Fisherman's Invocation* (poems) published (London: Heinemann).

1979   *The Fisherman's Invocation* receives British Commonwealth Poetry Prize (first African winner of the prize).

1982   Awarded Doctor of Letters (*Honoris Causa*), University of Port Harcourt.

1983   Death of Adhiambo Carmichael Okara, third wife, Port Harcourt.

1983–84   Invited lecturer on Ijaw culture, University of Port Harcourt.

1984   Board of Directors, Rivers State Council for Arts and Culture appointment.

1989   Contributes chapter to *Land and People of Rivers State*, ed. E. J. Alagoa. (Port Harcourt: Riverside Communications).

1990   "Towards the Evolution of an African Language for African Literature" (essay) published in *Kunapipi*, Department of English, University of Aarhus, Denmark.

1992   *Adventures to Juju Island* (children's story) published (Ibadan: Heinemann Educational Books).

"Continued Survival of Our Cultural Heritage" (essay) published in WAACLALS Lecture Series, ed. Ernest Emenyonu (Owerri: New Generation Books).

Receives Rivers State Government Merit Award.

1994   "The Role of Opinion Leaders: The Fight against Corruption" (paper) presented African Leadership Forum Conference in Benin Republic.

1995   Writer-in-residence, Alvan Ikoku College of Education, Owerri, Imo State.

"The Snowflakes Sail Gently Down" (reprinted) in *Concert of Voices: An Anthology of World Writing in English*, ed. V. J. Ramraj (Peterborough, Ontario: Broadview Press).

1996   Seminar on the author's work convened, University of Catania, Italy.

"Cultural and Linguistic Changes in Nigeria in the Past Thirty Years" (essay) published in seminar's collected papers.

1997   *Tonye and the Kingfish* (children's story) published (Port Harcourt: Beacon Press).

2000   "Metaphor of War" and "The Word, Poetic Vision and Society" (essays) published in *Goatskin, Bags, and Wisdom: New Critical Perspectives on African Literature*, ed. Ernest Emenyonu, (Trenton NJ: Africa World Press).

2001   Bayelsa State Government Merit Award; Officer of the Order of the Niger (OON); Federal Government of Nigeria National Award.

2004   *The Dreamer, His Vision* (poems) published (Port Harcourt: Port Harcourt University Press).

2005   Nigerian Liquefied Natural Gas (LNG) Prize for Poetry (joint recipient).

2006   *As I See It* (poems) published (Port Harcourt: Port Harcourt University Press).

Receives Award for Excellence in Creativity in African Literature (CALEL), University of Calabar.

"We Shared" (poem) published in *Of Minstrels and Masks: The Legacy of Ezenwa-Ohaeto in Nigerian Writing*, ed. Christine Matzke, Aderemi Raji-Oyelade, and Geoffrey V. Davis (Bloomington: Indiana University Press).

2007   *The Christmas Twins* (children's story) published (Yenagoa: Treasure Press).

"The Snowflakes Sail Gently Down," "Adhiambo," "Spirit of the Wind," "One Night at Victoria Beach" (poems) published in *The Penguin Book of Modern African Poetry*, ed. Gerald Moore and Ulli Beier (Harmondsworth UK: Penguin).

2009   Pan African Writers' Association Honorary Member Award.

2010   *Lion's Dilemma: Allegorical Fable of the African Present* (New York: Triatlantic Books).

Fellow of the Nigerian Academy of Letters (FNAL), (*Honoris Causa*).

2011   24 April, ninetieth birthday celebrations, Nigeria, Africa, and international literary communities.

To order or obtain more information on
these or other University of Nebraska
Press titles, visit nebraskapress.unl.edu.

CPSIA information can be obtained
at www.ICGtesting.com
Printed in the USA
LVHW110729270121
677554LV00005B/471

9 780803 286870

FRIEND OF
SINNERS

Douglas,
Many blessings,

FRIEND OF SINNERS

TAKING RISKS TO REACH THE LOST

Kelly M. Williams

CROSSLINK
PUBLISHING

Friend of Sinners: Taking Risks to Reach the Lost

P
Ꝑ CrossLink Publishing
www.crosslinkpublishing.com

Copyright © 2016 by Kelly M. Williams.

ISBN 978-1-63357-092-4

Library of Congress Control Number: 2016956721